GW00716373

COLLECTIVE LAW-BREAKING —
A THREAT TO LIBERTY

COLLECTIVE LAW-BREAKING —
A THREAT TO LIBERTY

EDITED BY CORINNE MICHAELA FLICK

CONVOCO! EDITIONS

Copyright © for the texts by the authors
and Convoco Foundation 2013

The rights of the named authors to be identified as the
authors of this work have been asserted in accordance
with the Copyright, Designs and Patents Act, 1988.

Convoco Foundation
Brienner Strasse 28
D-80333 Munich

www.convoco.co.uk

British Library Cataloguing-in-Publication Data: a catalogue
record for this book is available from the British Library.

Edited by Dr. Corinne Michaela Flick
Translated from German by Philippa Hurd
Layout and typesetting by Acorn Independent Press Ltd.

Printed in Great Britain

ISBN: 978-0-9572958-5-8

As the usages of society alter, the law must adapt itself to the various situations of mankind.

William Murray, Lord Mansfield (1705–93)

CONTENTS

CORINNE MICHAELA FLICK

INTRODUCTION

Dear Friends of Convoco,

The idea of this book is to call attention to the phenomenon of collective law-breaking, to its implications and dangers. We will be looking at law-breaking as committed by many people in the community all at the same time. This book evaluates the phenomenon, its motives, and its effects from different perspectives, summarizes these observations, and analyzes their relative contexts. I am delighted that I have been able to call upon so many thinkers from different disciplines to exchange ideas on this topic, to make connections between their ideas, and to form the individual elements into one overall picture. This holistic way of looking at issues is a new approach, and the only right method for dealing with today's problems. Only in this way can we face up to the complexity of our world.

Collective law-breaking is highly topical and touches our society at its very core. It encroaches upon many areas of law and life, without being consciously noticed by society. We can see that the sense of right and wrong within our society is changing. It is in the process of disintegrating. The individual's readiness to observe the rules is diminishing.

Our theme looks at law-breaking as social practice, as a cultural construct, and as a legally sanctionable activity. We will look at the question of whether collective law-breaking determines social change, or whether it is itself the result of changes going on in society.

Underpinning this are the following fundamental observations: what role does the law play in our collective life? What is the meaning of civil liberties? At what point does their erosion become a threat to freedom itself?

We will be looking at collective action by the state on the one hand, and collective action by individuals on the other, both as examples of law-breaking.

Collective law-breaking *at state level* becomes clear in the example of the Maastricht Treaty. Infringements of the Stability and Growth Pact have now become too many to count. The reasons for this are various: vague and thus impracticable legal concepts, such as for example macroeconomic equilibrium derived from the German Stability and Growth Law on the one hand; and on the other legally precise regulations that, as they cannot be applied unambiguously, are frequently not deployed.

Vague legal concepts and political interests mislead us into making decisions based on opportunism. Thus the bailout clause in Article 125 of the Treaty on the Functioning of the European Union (TFEU), which can be interpreted in several different ways, is the cause of controversy over the original financial aid offered to Greece, and the European Central Bank's purchase of government bonds.

On September 12, 2012 Germany's Federal Constitutional Court delivered its verdict on the controversial Fiscal Pact and the European Stability Mechanism (ESM). Courts are called upon to define what is the law. Not just Germany, but the entire European community is unsettled.

It is debatable whether the Maastricht Treaty was ever intended to be observed. The practical impossibility of fulfilling its convergence criteria suggests that when the Treaty was signed only a formal observance was expected. But this loses the true meaning and purpose of a contract. Fulfillment is the aim of every contract, and is a categorical imperative.

The famous principle of *pacta sunt servanda* represents a categorical imperative. But it is taken as a guiding principle less and less frequently. Contracting parties come to an understanding without the will to commit themselves. In signing the contract they do not safeguard their own interests sufficiently. But self-interest constitutes the motivation necessary to abide by the fulfillment of an agreement.

What this means in the case of Europe is the following: the attraction of the union lies in the fact that it enables one to discover other cultures and languages. Europe brings together differences, and ensures a diversity that becomes productive in union. This unity is underpinned by the signing of treaties and by agreements. The benefits of this cultural mosaic only pertain if these treaties and agreements are observed. Thus Europe should be a union that distinguishes itself through the observance of contracts.

However, it is not merely the case that contracts are not being observed; laws are being broken as well.

Infringements of the law as a result of *the behavior of individuals* are now common in the areas of data protection and copyright.

The virtual world of the Internet poses a challenge to the law as it stands. For example, the illegal downloading of content from the Internet is regarded as a minor offence. Downloading, streaming, copying—the free use of content seems to have become socially acceptable. The fact that this is an attack on intellectual property rights and a threat to the existence of entire sectors of the economy seems to be of very little interest.

Online companies infringe data protection guidelines by using their economic power simply to flout them. Nevertheless users avail themselves of these companies' services—against their own legitimate interests. How do companies arrive at the point where they believe that they can continue to break the law? And why do consumers look the other way when faced with such illegal behavior? Today the user is the only person who might be able to punish wrongdoing. This is the case not only in the online world. In other areas too, such as climate protection or scarcity of resources, it is the individual who wields the power. The citizen is the one person who can have an influence on the system through his or her own behavior.

Beyond this, collective law-breaking takes place in other areas: tax evasion and illegal employment are cited as examples.

At this point another question arises: is it legal to combat law-breaking using illegal means? That is, exposing illegal activity (tax evasion) by equally illegal activity (hacking or the purchase of data that has been acquired by illegal means)? In this case, it is argued that the end justifies the means.

Today action is often dependent on the notion that the observance of the rules would make the situation worse. This opens the way to law-breaking. Again and again there are calls for deregulation. Such calls are to a large extent characteristic of what society thinks today. We must not forget that behind this demand lies the desire to impose one's own will and thus one's own advantage. Deregulation—it is often overlooked—is in the last analysis the basis of arbitrary behavior. Ultimately the stronger party wins through, and in such a society the public good is no longer paramount. The *bonum commune* cited by Caesar and Cicero is lost.

We should be aware that while the law is the basis of power on the one hand, on the other it also sets the limits of power. The law forms a horizontally negotiated relationship between the citizen and the state or states. Whoever acknowledges regulations and treaties votes against a vertical power structure.

All this presumes, however, that the law is valid. If the law is to prevail, it requires the acknowledgment of rules. This assumes that the individual understands that laws are the indispensable foundation of cooperation. It is important to recognize that it is in the individual's self-interest to submit to regulations. For even if such rules restrict his or her own sovereignty, they are the guarantee of protection and security. Only if one is aware of the function of the law, can one recognize how dangerous it is not to observe laws, thereby eroding them insidiously. In the last analysis the state loses its monopoly on power on the one hand, and on the other its power is not limited and moderated by the law. The freedom of the individual is not guaranteed. And thus the state founded on the rule of law is abandoned.

Of course at this juncture we should consider how far the law should adapt to society. The law is an organic structure, which means that it changes and adapts. Its orientation towards society and society's needs must be paramount. The law can only fulfill its civilizing role when it reflects the ethical and moral requirements of a society, and both reflects and works alongside technical, social, and societal changes. A legal system cannot be allowed to ossify. Only then can we expect observance of the law—that is the individual's fundamental preparedness to acknowledge the law.

However, this aim or adjustment takes place equally—though not exclusively—through collective law-breaking. The latter makes us aware of a discrepancy or estrangement. It is important that collective infringement of the law does not take the place of observance of the law. It should not be allowed to spread like an epidemic, while at the same time being ignored by society. For law means security, justice, and peace.

Corinne Michaela Flick
London, March 2013

THESES

Wolfgang Schön

The concept of democracy suggests a correspondence between normative collective will and actual collective action. But when law is handed over to state institutions, the threat of collective law-breaking increases. This can be a sign of social progress, but can also appear as a constitutionally alarming lack of law enforcement. The state should aim at a correspondence between norm and action, either by pursuing the implementation of the diktat of norms "educationally", or by wisely abandoning the notion of perfect normative standards. It is crucial that the legal system remain credible and does not lose consistency over the course of time.

Corinne Michaela Flick

It is important to recognize that it is in the individual's self-interest to submit to regulations that restrict his or her personal sovereignty, but which offer protection and security in exchange. The law can only fulfill its civilizing role when it reflects the ethical and moral requirements of a society, and both reflects and works alongside technical, social, and societal changes. Only then can we expect observance of the law.

Hannes Siegrist and Pirmin Stekeler-Weithofer

The reasons for collective law-breaking are to a great degree determined by the historical context as well as the horizon of meaning and standpoint of the actors. Examples of collective law-breaking can be necessary for the development of human rights. But they can also damage the foundations of individual and collective human rights. In many cases their significance remains ambivalent. It is one of the tasks of philosophy and history to analyze systematically, conceptually, critically, and empirically the social and cultural preconditions, forms, and consequences of collective law-breaking.

Christoph G. Paulus

Examples of collective law-breaking have existed since ancient times. Seneca recognized that the larger the number of perpetrators, the more lacking in scruples the individual becomes. The law is clearly an inalienable desideratum of human society. Anthropologically and sociologically it has an undisputed *raison d'être*. However legal history teaches us that the law may not stray too far from what is socially acceptable if it wants to be observed.

This implies an understanding of the "substance of the law" that says that the law should be observed just because it is the law. If a citizen can make a distinction between the law as enshrined in statute and what he perceives to be the law, then the law is no longer identical with its mandatory observance. The result is collective law-breaking.

Shaukat Aziz

The root of the problem the world is facing today lay in a lack of regulation in complex areas of the financial industry. However, the fact is that the problems that led to the crisis were being uncovered and dealt with in countries that are constantly undergoing critical examination. It is the mark of a mature citizenry that its members are able to look themselves collectively in the mirror, and honestly identify their own faults as a society, rather than blame their problems on others. The desire for constant progress, development, and improvement is the hallmark of a mature, democratic society.

Ingolf Pernice

Collective law-breaking means that factual behavior opposes the kind of behavior that is expected under the rule of law. It requires a certain degree of commonality of purpose between several law-breakers. Collective law-breaking has no meaning in law, but it does have a social and therefore a political meaning.

At a European level we identify collective law-breaking in the disregard of obligations that the governments of the Member States imposed upon themselves under the Maastricht Treaty. The Member States should have honored the trust they had placed in the observance of the law in order to prevent the edifice of Maastricht from collapsing. Today the financial crisis in Europe demonstrates the devastating consequences that collective law-breaking can have.

The law cannot protect us from collective law-breaking. Defending the regulating effect of the law and its observance is the task of the individual and lies in all our interests. The law is the condition of freedom, just as a functioning economic and monetary union is a prerequisite for the protection of assets in Europe.

Jürgen Stark

The regulatory principles of the economic and monetary union have not only been treated in a lax manner, they have been disregarded. These principles were regarded as formulae that could be interpreted flexibly, and not as central regulatory stipulations. Principles and rules that should be regarded as guidelines for political action at all times and not only in "fair weather" were regarded as onerous, as they restrict the political sphere of maneuver. But it is precisely during times of crisis that such principles should provide some orientation in the medium term. We can see here clear differences in legal understanding and sense of right and wrong between the Member States and within the European institutions.

Roland Berger

A way out of the crisis and the state of illegality is offered by a politically monitored but privately financed growth program that will create, strengthen, and modernize Europe's infrastructure. The job of the politicians, I suggest, would be to bring these infrastructure needs together with the investment requirements of private capital.

Every general program of "just saving", every austerity program always goes hand in hand with recession and its consequences such as unemployment, devaluation of assets, increasing social security costs, even to the extent of social unrest.

WOLFGANG SCHÖN
THE LIMITS OF LAW ENFORCEMENT

"Between what is and what should be—societies that break their own law as a threat to our liberty" is the topic of the Convoco lectures in 2012. And it is a puzzling one. Not only are the legal problems hidden within this topic a cause for concern, it is already puzzling in the way it is formulated. What does "collective law-breaking" actually mean? Is it not a *contradictio in adjecto*? Is it not the collective itself that defines what should ultimately be accepted as law? For both the layman and the specialist law appears to be the "rule" not only in the sense of the normativity of a regulation, but also in the sense of a positive description of what is done regularly, how one behaves under normal conditions. By contrast, law-breaking, one might think, always presents an exception. It is the case of the individual, who adopts a position against the collective through his unlawful conduct. Thus "collective law-breaking" appears to be something that does not exist at all.

This fundamental understanding of the law as the statistically normative rule is derived from many sources. As early as Roman law the recognition of traditional legal norms was based on the *communis opinio*, the general concept shared by fair and equitable-thinking people. Since Rousseau the idea of the social contract has been linked to the notion that the general consensus of a nation is the foundation of its constitution and legal system. And in our era the American philosopher of law John Rawls traces the legal framework of community life back to the principles on which all members of a community can agree as a rational set of rules under the "veil of ignorance" (that is without knowing anything about one's personal future situation). The concept of democracy—of "government of the people, by the people, and for the people" (Abraham Lincoln)— suggests a pre-stabilized agreement between collective will and collective action.

A rift between what is and what should be as agreed by the collective can always arise if we hand responsibility for the law over to institutions. This occurs if a constitution emerges encompassing democratically legitimized institutions that produce a binding definition of the form and content of the legal system—a definition that is binding for all members of the collective. And such a rift threatens to open up when these legal regulations— from constitutional law via simple law of statute to secondary guidelines in the form of by-laws, regulations, and administrative provisions—enter into conflict with social movements, trends, and public opinions, with the image that sections of the collective have of themselves within the larger collective, sections that do not want to come to terms with the institutionally created consensus. Thus our theme can be defined as the conflict between regulatory law as the product of constitutional, i.e. democratically and constitutionally legitimized institutions on the one hand, and vague, countervailing trends in social groups that are difficult to gauge in their size and significance on the other.

The second puzzle in this topic resides in the phrase "threat to our liberty." Who actually is this "we"? What in fact is the major collective, in opposition to which a perhaps somewhat smaller collective plays the role of law-breaker? Our first thought, of course, is to look to society as the community of those who are members of a state. But the quality of internal homogeneity is disappearing more and more from this society. There is little on which a modern, western society can really still agree. In addition processes of migration can lead to the formation within a society of sections of the collective who no longer fundamentally accept certain rules as a matter of course. Thus it is important to re-define the overarching collective as well, this self-evident "we." Perhaps we should re-define it as a "nation built upon principles" in Abraham Lincoln's sense of the phrase, as a community of common values, as a society of "constitutional patriots" (Dolf Sternberger) and therefore also of "legal patriots."

In the formulation of our topic the word "liberty" appears particularly elegant. For a lot of what we observe today in collective law-breaking seems to be directed against abstractions, against prevailing relationships, against the state in general, and against the power of economic monopolies. At first glance there is a lack of damage to the individual, of tangible losses, and thus too in the case of state authorities a lack of feeling for the lasting effects of these examples of law-breaking. However, collective infringement of abstract norms can merge insidiously into an invasion of individual rights, into an assault on the individual person. And that means that in this conflict the small collective is not only opposed to the large one, but also law-breaking by a section of the collective is opposed to "vested rights", that is, opposed to the constitutional security of every individual.

Can this broad area of conflict be mapped? Can we identify cases that make systematic access and analytical clarity possible? In what follows we will present various constellations to this end, constellations where what is and what should be, social consensus and state regulation on a collective basis, fall apart. The nature of the problem and the possibilities for its solution will be seen to be very different in each case.

Let us start with cases in which social developments precede state developments. Anyone who knows the German legislation on sex offences during the 1950s, for example the provisions covering procuration and homosexuality, will see relatively clearly, in my opinion, that these are areas in which a broad-based social consensus has over the course of decades outstripped the traditional requirements of the law. These norms, formally abolished by state legislators in the 1970s, actually persisted only in a negligible form, which was scarcely ever enforced and which was no longer accepted by society as a whole.

Such cases must exist and will always exist, as a society requires openness in order to experiment. In relation to this, Friedrich von Hayek said that this is where the boundary between law and morality exists. A moral law is based on the assumption that the mass of the population conforms to it, but it allows the individual to break with tradition and risk experimentation. The law may not be conceived in such a way that it stands in the way of this kind of social change.

Related to this, but with a different thrust, is a form of legal disobedience that appears in the form of protest and thus comes up against social processes. In this case, law-breaking does not appear as a veiled resistance to social norms, but as a transparent attempt to move society and its institutions forward. The demonstrations of the 1960s as well as the sit-ins of the 1970s belong to this category. Today we can perhaps add to this the events surrounding the Castor transports.[1] Insofar as private rights are infringed or situations liable to result in criminal proceedings occur, this is of course law-breaking that must be prosecuted. But this is an extraordinary case which, due to its public impact and its political significance, clearly deserves extraordinary and separate consideration.

Both the above-mentioned cases—moral progress and political protest—describe situations in which society is, as it were, one step ahead of the law of the state. But the reverse also exists. There is also the situation in which the state deliberately creates laws in order to establish new social standards—perhaps even new moral standards. This is what my colleague Christoph Engel from the Max-Planck-Institut in Bonn in his research on collective goods calls "educational state action." The state as teacher—is that not an old legal entity in the philosophy of law?

Let us look at the example of environmental protection: in the 1970s concerns about "natural resources" were not yet widely accepted in society, but legislators gave them normative force. An example is the development of the catalytic converter for gasoline engines. Initially the state employed both carrot and stick, that is tax breaks as well as coercive measures, in order to establish environmentally sound standard equipment in this area. Today I assume there is a broad social consciousness about the environment that would encourage most citizens buying a car to ask for catalytic converters of their own volition. Another example is the introduction of anti-trust legislation in the 1950s. At the time the German corporate landscape, which was extremely cartel-friendly since the time of Walther Rathenau, was forcibly liberalized under pressure from US politicians by means of the law against competition restrictions. The cartel agreement, which was clearly still actionable and enforceable during the Weimar period, was robbed of its effectiveness under civil law and made subject to heavy penalties. This took place against a backdrop of persistent opposition from German industry, but now forms part of the current status of our free economic system that we take for granted. A final example of "educational state action" can be seen in the rise of capital markets law over the last few decades. Twenty years ago insider trading was regarded as a mere minor offence, yet today it is prosecuted in law and sanctions against the practice are generally accepted. Directors must declare their share dealings in businesses that they lead, and the secretiveness of boards of directors has now given way to ad hoc disclosures. The state is leading the way over and above society like a strict pedagogue.

Matters become more complicated when new technologies present the law with new challenges. Many young people come across the question of what the difference is between right and wrong perhaps for the first time when downloading music illegally. Is it permitted to download the latest tracks for free from an anonymous foreign website? The legal system has a clear answer in cases of copyright protection. But a social consensus has not yet been arrived at with regard to such questions. Equally there exists no comprehensive technical means of monitoring this. In this instance can we say this is merely a case of a practical lack of sanctions against gross injustice, or is this an example of the creation of a new social norm? The Pirate Party tries to maintain that this is a case of social progress and civil disobedience—not merely a case of hidden consumption comparable to shoplifting, but the start of something new, of a world of what we call in the scientific landscape open access to information.

Equally it is not easy to assess cases in which the law always already existed, but its consistent enforcement was lacking, with the result that a wide-reaching disobedience developed in the past. A frequently cited example is the area of tax fraud. Thirty years ago the avoidance of overseas tax was not only often perceived as a minor offence, but the state did not even really pursue it. Many people sensed an unspoken consensus between citizens and the state: "we declare nothing and you do nothing." Leading academics described the taxation of capital investments as a "tax on stupidity" and complained individually against the failure of the authorities to take action. It was the German Constitutional Court, in its 1991 decision on the taxation of savings income, that ultimately put the financial authorities under enormous pressure to enact "equality of application," and thus a movement was set in train that is still ongoing today.

Parallel to the change in state intervention, there is now also a change in the way society regards these crimes. This reveals a considerable problem of transformation: how does one move from collective law-breaking to collective observance of the law? This brings us to the tragic situation that the state, in attempting to counteract the collective law-breaking of its citizens, employs means (for example, buying stolen CDs containing data on rich tax evaders) that legally, or at least morally appear highly questionable. One wrong countering another: that is no basis for a functioning tax system. In such a situation collective law-breaking must be tackled using collective tools, whether by means of amnesties, or by means of agreements to allow the possibility of drawing a line under past events and establishing a new equilibrium.

Common to the cases described here is that social behavior across the board, perhaps not always collectively in the sense of agreed behavior, but still collective in the sense of behavior on a mass scale, deviates from the requirements of the state legal system. Things are different once again if states work together as collectives and disregard the laws that bind them together. Today the subsidies provided by the Euro states and the European Central Bank during the fiscal crisis affecting southern Europe are frequently attacked as collective law-breaking. Meanwhile the infringement of the no-bailout principle in the European treaties has been a topic addressed even by the German Constitutional Court itself. In addition we might mention the collective intervention by western military powers in Kosovo and Iraq which was undertaken without sufficient cause in support of a UN Security Council decision. Is this too a case of unlawful collective action that might demand closer scrutiny?

In the case of collective law-breaking it is usual that the law demands more severe, more targeted, and more thorough enforcement, that is an enforcement that is more equal under the law. But as a result of such a demand, do we not end up with a state that might itself constitute a "threat to our liberty"—the state as executioner or a police state?

Take this example: who still remembers that ten years ago the German Finance Minister Hans Eichel announced that he intended to send representatives of the social services and the tax office into private homes in order to search for anyone who was employed illegally? This threat was quickly withdrawn, as there was no social consensus for this kind of intervention into the private sphere. In such a situation should the state change its approach from the stick back to the carrot, from sanctions to positive incentives? Let us once again take the example of domestic working conditions. A few years ago tax legislators decided to introduce a way of making the costs involved in such work partly tax deductible: this was an incentive towards law-abiding behavior which brings domestic staff within the tax and social security systems, thus possibly having a stronger effect than the use of policing in solving the problem, which is only effective in individual cases.

Occasionally there are answers to the problem where society itself, the market, and its citizens provide the solutions. For example, with its iTunes offer Apple managed to make legal downloading of music so easily available at low cost that both state and parents can easily demand that their offspring remain law-abiding. In this way lawful behavior no longer means going without the enjoyment of music.

The situation becomes really difficult if collective law-breaking continues for a long time without both state and market finding an appropriate means of enforcement. In this case the state must inevitably ask whether it should withdraw. What kind of legislation is so essential that its enforcement must be ensured at all costs? When could even an incomplete enforcement be justified both legally and politically? Sometimes it is necessary to have the maximum application of the law, and a ridiculously detailed amount of legislation, for example in employment protection, in food safety regulations, and in safety technology. We value the fact that the Road Traffic Act provides reliable and accurate specifications that a heavy goods vehicle must follow to be permitted on our roads, or if medicines are subject to exhaustive licensing procedures. And in any case the practice of the law should not be allowed to descend into formulaic responses. Many of the requirements that establish modern codes of corporate governance for businesses appear problematic. Here we can see an emerging tendency towards a commercial law comprised of secondary virtues.

In many cases obligations to provide information and rules on documentation are a distraction from concentrating on a business's core activities. There is a law in the world of football that perhaps could also be applied to business life: he who knows the rules best doesn't win the game.

Once again the state authorities must clarify how far one can regulate on this matter. Above all legislators must hold back from introducing unrealistic expectations, whether it is stability criteria in the Maastricht Treaty or the legal expectation of a place at nursery school: the state should not introduce any regulations whose political enforceability, when it comes to the crunch, is not assured. The legal system must remain credible, and must fulfill the requirement that economists call time consistency. And above all what Josef Isensee warned about years ago at a seminar in Bonn must not happen: a constitution may not be conceived in such a way that an economic crisis can suddenly turn into a constitutional crisis. Such prudence among legislators is also necessary to ensure that the normative force and the stabilizing effect of the really central provisions of our legal system are not eroded by people not obeying the law in many less significant contexts.

Perhaps other ways of solving this problem also include the introduction of new democratic processes, and the extension of grass-roots participation. From a constitutional and political point of view we can say that the frequently encountered difference between society's expectations and institutionally legitimized laws can be overcome through new forms of grass-roots participation.

In conclusion, there is no sense in bewailing the loss of legal principles, solidarity, or morality. There are indeed examples demonstrating an improvement in social attitudes, for instance in the field of the environment, in questions of economic and political transparency, and in the areas of corruption and tax evasion. The improvement in the standard of behavior over the last few years was partly guided by legislators, and partly emerged from society itself.

For me, it is more important at this juncture to raise once again the question of who is this "us", this "we". Solidarity with and in a legal system leads to the question: how comprehensively can one actually conceive of a collective of individuals and still be able to guarantee internal stability? In this context economists talk about optimal club size. We are not suggesting a return to a 19th-century small-state mentality; this would be no match for the demands of globalization. In my opinion, the constitutional state of the Federal Republic of Germany forms the minimum size for a stable society. The real question is whether Europe as a whole is already stable and efficient enough in its current size to serve as the benchmark of social and state solidarity? Or must we go further and form international collectives? We might think of climate change, where it has taken a long time to create a kindred sense of right and wrong with global agreement. This may seem Utopian, but perhaps the scale of the problem also demands large-scale answers.

What is to be done if in a concrete situation the requirements of the law and the coercive effect of the facts result in a completely unbridgeable divide? Is the European financial crisis just such a case, when a strict adherence to the provisions of the European Treaties threatens to tear the European Union apart? No one wants to utter the phrase *fiat iustitia pereat mundus.* But a simple attitude of "there is no alternative" with regard to the constraints cannot allow us to ignore normative requirements. For the lawyers the main principle of a steady advance towards the most legally correct position prevails. This advance may take the form of a change in the quality of enforcement, or it can even lie in reducing the normative impact of the law in less important situations. By this I mean not so much an objective concept, and more a subjective attitude. For the lawyers there remains what Roman law already acknowledged as the core of justice, that is the *constans et perpetua voluntas, ius suum cuique tribuendi,* the constant and perpetual will to render to every man his due. This will must never be forgotten.

Note

1. These events are protests against recycled German nuclear waste which is transported from France to Gorleben in Germany in containers known as Castors. [Translator's note.]

HANNES SIEGRIST AND PIRMIN STEKELER-WEITHOFER

RECOGNITION PROBLEMS IN POSITIVE LAW AND ITS DELICATE RELATIONSHIP WITH FREEDOM

1. Sanctions-based Law and a Notion of Ethics based on Freedom

At first sight the theme of "collective law-breaking as a threat to liberty" is confusing. On the one hand any breach of the law is ultimately a threat to liberty, in any case, insofar as we can suppose, with Thomas Hobbes[1] and G.W.F. Hegel,[2] for example, *that (positive) law is the constitutive framework of any social freedom within a state.* Ultimately this means the law in any form of state or society where it guarantees a certain degree of security of life and limb, of property or even of ownership, and moreover determines the realm of freedom of individuals in society. For this very reason we can consider entire states and societies, each according to the constitution of their positive law, as more or less based on freedom.

In any case the following applies apparently as a matter of course: the more people break the law, the greater the dangers to personal freedom, which always of course includes security in how people organize their lives and actions.

However, collective law-breaking becomes a special problem in the particular areas of tax law, economic behavior such as corruption or insider trading, or in the area of laws designed to protect intellectual property, which are also always laws of copy protection. In all these cases it is not always immediately possible to monitor the observance of laws and their infringements, with the result that we have to rely on a certain amount of voluntary *compliance*. The problem becomes clear if we think of the requirements of tax inspection. Such inspection is necessary in order to combat inclinations towards tax evasion at least to a certain extent by means of deterrence, as such tendencies arise structurally as attractive possibilities for the individual simply because a tax declaration is a free declaration. Because of this there arises the problem that a fair tax system presupposes a certain honesty among taxpayers, while at the same time however the recognition of the entire tax regime and the state that administers it. The fact that this actually is a problem is still not taken seriously by some states, even including some EU members. The purchase of CDs containing the data of illegal tax evaders shows clearly that it is also a problem for the citizens of Germany.[3]

We are aware of other instances where control measures against the possible abuse of free, honest behavior are necessary from the case of public transport, from legal proceedings against the trade in pirated goods which have recently been in the news, but also from the growing need for control measures internal to companies, known as *compliance*. The meaning of this concept can be defined thus:[4] "The concept of compliance describes the totality of all reasonable measures that underpin the regulation-compliant behavior of a company, of its management and supervisory bodies, and of its members with regard to all legal requirements and prohibitions."[5] The theme of compliance has been topical since 2001 at the latest, that is since the Enron scandal, and the long-term global crisis in finance and the stock market. Thus it is certainly not just a fashionable theme, although it is also that, as the existence of at least two German-language journals on this subject demonstrates.[6]

One of Vladimir Ilyich Lenin's most famous dictums says: "Trust is good, control is better." And indeed this dictum articulates a fundamental problem in positive law: for such a law cannot only be determined by a subject matter that tells us what is to be done, what is to be refrained from, and what is legal or permitted according to the law. It is also always necessary for there to be state underpinning of the law through the threat of sanctions, which also motivates those people who would not do this of their own free will based on a sense of civic virtue or morality to be guided by the law in their actions. Only a law based on sanctions is a true law of right. If an action is exempt from punishment—for example abortion before the third month of pregnancy, even in the absence of special circumstances—then, if one nevertheless considers this "illegal," it is simply a question of a moralistic appeal to a misguided kind of law. In the interests of social harmony or to counter moralistic concerns and concerns motivated by Christianity, it can make sense to enact even such pseudo laws. In this case, however, a collective breach of the law by women would not only not be a danger to freedom, it is not even clear what one means when we say that this is a breach of the law.

"The problem of organizing a state…can be solved even for a race of devils," writes Kant, in a phrase that is as dramatic as it is profound, in order to express the idea that the law of the state backed by sanctions, which is enforceable with the threat of punishment in the case of infringements of the law, can be seen as necessary and useful even by a pure *homo economicus*. For only the deferral of the expected system of pay-offs through the state-supported threat of punishment and the punishment that then actually ensues from the violation of the threat induce many people to act as the law requires. Hobbes discusses this through the example of theft. In the case of theft it is the attraction of theft in the first place that can lead even as far as murder in order to protect the theft: the dead man can no longer avenge himself. And he can no longer name the perpetrators. Thus we need other people to avenge the murdered man, that is to threaten the potential murderer with revenge in advance. Thus the blood feud pursued by family groups is altogether an early form of law, even if it is a double-edged institution, as we know. Ultimately it was replaced with criminal prosecution by the state, and the blood feud itself is now considered one of the most serious crimes. The notion that "there is no such thing as a free lunch" applies not only in economics, but also in institutional affairs. All rules entail costs, even if these costs "only" exist in the possibility of the abuse of the state's powers of sanction or in their failure.

Even for Hobbes the dramatic example of theft, murder, and the spiral of revenge is used to make clear to us in a paradigmatic way the general means by which the expected benefit of an action is redirected by means of law, threat of punishment, and punishment. In terms of subject matter nothing really essential has been added in the more recent presentations of the problem of collective economic action, for example in the well-known example of the prisoner's dilemma.

The prisoner's dilemma shows how not only threats of punishment but also promises can change the system of pay-offs. A state prosecutor makes each of two suspects in the same murder case a legal offer of leniency. If only one "grasses" on the other, the "grass" gets a suspended sentence. The grassed-up suspect gets ten years. If both betray each other, they both get five years. If both say nothing, they both get a year. The *homo economicus* or "rational" egotist who does not openly trust the other person, can in this case only betray the other. For if he says nothing he runs the risk of the other person grassing on him. More precisely he thinks like this: if the other man says nothing and I betray him, I'll go free, which is better than a year in prison. If the other man "talks" it's also better if I "talk." A mere five years in prison is better than ten years. As both men think like this, they will both betray each other and both get five years. The prosecuting attorney's bill goes up. However, now we have the feeling that the rationality of the *homo rationalis economicus* is nowhere near as rational as it appears. And in fact, as Plato tried to show Socrates, and in turn Kant showed, for him, without morality and trust a good life is simply not possible.

On the other hand ever since Plato's analyses in *The Republic [Politeia]* and the *Laws [Nomoi]* we also know that the state is necessary as an authority of law and sanction. Trusting in free cooperations, merely supported by a verbal, moral faculty of judgment and the free boycotts which possibly result from this in the case of a breach of trust, as might happen in small family groups, are insufficient for the functioning of larger societies with their complex division of labor and allocation of resources. Thus Plato's *Republic* and *Laws*, despite all the criticism of details, are a model for all later philosophies of the state and of law, and for the political and social sciences in their discussion of the basic problems of human cooperation and the division of labor.

However, the question of what can be legislated for at all in law and can be reinforced by means of state sanctions, and what by contrast can be left to free cooperation (or free non-cooperation), underpinned merely by a sense of morality, offers a starting point for a complex interdisciplinary diagnosis of our present condition. Of course that would be a wide area, if it in fact also encompassed the whole other, parallel and perhaps much deeper and thus also much more complex question of collective *breach of trust* through *non-moral* actions as a threat to our liberty. Nevertheless, Niklas Luhmann wrote a book on the theme of "trust,"[7] although he is probably too lacking in radicalism in his recognition that a free society is not possible without trust, so that in the end Lenin's dictum turns out to be false if it is not restricted quite closely to particular cases. Monitoring everything that goes on in human cooperation and the division of labor, and thus also in economic activity, and subjugating it all in advance to legislation and a regime of sanctions, is simply not possible.

This might suffice to justify the restriction of our theme to that of the law. In the first place, therefore, we will leave the problems of the "soft norms" of free morality and free cooperation behind us, even if they are still regarded as the "poor relation" in a social, economic, cultural, and legal narrative, precisely because what is implicitly obvious cannot, like what has already been articulated as a rule, be the immediate subject of positive research. General education in society about what is ethically implicit is thus still necessary even today particularly in the historical social sciences.

2. Collective Law-Breaking as the Non-Recognition of a Norm

There exist collective breaches of the law that not only present no threat to liberty but that have advanced and still do advance civil rights in the face of abuses of the legal system that are partly paternalistic, and partly group-led and moralistic, in order to promote a provincial sense of morality for instance. As examples we might think of the long-term struggles against Section 175 of the German Penal Code [which prohibited male homosexuality] or even against Section 180 which represents an outmoded form of legal protection for young people and marriage. But the battle over the legalization of abortions up to a certain term, which is still not resolved, also belongs in this category: how the laws protecting unborn life remain controversial for various reasons, not least because it is always about a regionally specific legal codification of an implicitly handed-down and religiously influenced sexual ethic and morality about procreation. The latter always also become part of the development of a society's morality, distilling ethics and law from particular religious traditions. Moreover, if we look at the general rhetoric of this example more closely, the foundations of the argument are astonishingly inconsistent, for instance in the discourse surrounding the protection of (unborn) life. For in a certain sense sperm too are alive—from which clearly (and hopefully) there is still no derivation of property law. Somewhat less frivolous is the following observation: no one talks about protecting the life of *brain-dead* patients, although these people are undoubtedly still alive. However, since here the utilitarian notion that one can help other people through organ donation outweighs the idea of protecting life even among a majority of Christians, no one has any objection to the "deliberate killing" of brain-dead patients for the purposes of organ donation. Quite the opposite: there is a massive moralistic campaign in favor of people in society offering their own body for organ donation. Of course permission must be given, as otherwise the extraction of organs would be punishable by law, even when usually this is justified not by the "life" of the brain-dead patient but by his autonomy in relation to his ability to dispose of his body both before and after death. In this instance, therefore, appeal is made to "honoring" the dead, which does not fit this case terribly well as the dead person is still alive. Indeed a revised definition of the moment of death using the criterion of brain death does not solve the problem. Physiologically the brain-dead individual is not dead, and the metabolism would go on living if one continued to feed the individual.

The examples show that collective non-recognition of traditional legal and moral norms does not always have to be a threat to our liberty or to the freedom of society as a whole. This brings us to a closer examination of the role of the law and in particular the function and meaning of human rights in a dynamic, modern, and open society. In this context, at least, it will be enough to pose these few questions:

• What forms of social wilfulness, cultural resistance, and deviant behavior lie at the roots of collective law-breaking?

• In the case of collective law-breaking, to what extent is it a question of transient and exceptional phenomena that are determined by the inadequate or delayed adjustment or synchronization of the law with social, cultural, and technical possibilities and developments, for example?

• To what extent are collective breaches of the law the consequence of a loss of coherence in and a limited monitoring of existing legislation? This can happen, for example, in times of far-reaching, accelerated change and the breakdown of society in the age of globalization.

• In that case, however, when do collective breaches of the law appear as symptoms of a more far-reaching and general social "anomie", i.e. of a general loss of regulation or of lawlessness which has its roots in the multiplicity of, competition between, and inconsistency of existing laws and moral requirements?

• At what point will the informalization and pluralization of laws be perceived, conceived, and sanctioned as an erosion of human rights and of the social, political, and legal order?

• How are collective breaches of the law, that can be understood as phenomena of a more or less profound legal and institutional crisis and of social change, both halted and domesticated, for example from the point of view of guaranteeing human rights?

• When can we understand and explain collective breaches of the law as the expression or even the motor of historical processes of development and social change? What relationship does the concept of and discourse surrounding "collective law-breaking" have to general discourses on the current and future nature of society?

3. Threats to Society

Of course some acts of collective law-breaking threaten a free democracy in a particular way. An example is collective tax evasion which can, through its effect on the national budget, ruin a country's entire economy, for example that of Greece. In addition there is illegal employment and collective abuse of the welfare systems, as well as other kinds of free-riding behavior. In our own societies, many central services and a lot of infrastructure work are ultimately organized by the state. This is why a breakdown in the public sector has such a drastic effect on a society's economy, and threatens the freedom of action of all members of society. This occurs in democracies when they do not realize, as in the case of the prisoner's dilemma, that one's own social conditions deteriorate specifically when one maximizes one's own immediate benefits privately. It is almost like a satire occurring in real life: on the one hand one associates Greece with the great political thinkers of antiquity—Sophocles, Plato, and Aristotle—but at the same time we can see that nothing of their insights remains, apart from the widespread but unjustified claim to be part of this same tradition.

"Family" oriented communities based on patronage, such as exist in the Mediterranean, Christian Orthodox, and also in the Islamic cultural traditions are clearly particularly susceptible to nepotistic and Mafia-like structures. From this observation emerges the not insignificant insight that it is precisely the overestimation of the economic potential of moral communitarianism or of a moral system created by analogy with the family that endangers a society's freedom. Collective law-breaking can often be traced back to a correspondingly ambivalent attitude towards the state on the one hand, and towards what we call morality on the other. People appeal verbally to morality and honesty, altruism and solidarity, but do not want to implement the substance of the issue in a publicly monitored way, withdrawing their simple voluntary compliance through the use of sanctions.

Even Plato tried in vain to combat nepotism through his ideas of anti-familial educational institutions. To this end, as we know, young people were to be removed from their parents' houses. Marriage was to be completely abolished, with the result that no one might know any more who was related to whom, and thus, in Plato's Utopia, everyone might feel related to everyone else. Of course this is unrealistic. As a diagnosis, however, it indicates a serious problem.

Just as ambivalent as Mafia-style nepotism in family-oriented societies was collective law-breaking in states based on "cooperative" principles, that is in former Eastern bloc countries whose socialism was conceived as overly communitarian (based on morality and the family). Long before the end of this kind of socialism in 1989 the motto "we are the people," that is the belief in public property, was taken so literally that people appropriated everything they could for their own private use. In practice a form of un-solidarity with the community arose, and a result of this was the economic decline of these states, which led ironically, via their collapse, to their freedom.

Once again we can see that this theme always leads back to the question of the relationship between free "moral" responsibility and a formal, legal system (a theme that was already of interest to Plato in his *Republic*, and is still being debated in the work of Niklas Luhmann today). And it leads to the question about the tense relationship between merely verbal and real solidarity as practised by people within a society.

It is interesting to look at Plato's story in Book VIII of the *Republic* which describes the decline of a good republican society that replaces an ethic of freedom with the striving for private glory and private wealth. Today we would add that a "democracy" tends to be threatened by the "plutocratic" inclinations of all individuals to make themselves richer, particularly civil servants. This leads Plato back to the delicate role played by a notion of "ethics" or "morality" based on freedom in a fully functional (indeed even democratic) republic.

Moreover the role of collective recognition of the state and of its laws aimed at freedom and solidarity in a society is particularly interesting. This recognition cannot be made clear in words alone, but must also appear through actions. Here there can be a contradiction between the words and deeds not only of individuals, but also within the collective. This means that an entire country can deceive itself about its supposed coherence and solidarity as a national population and as a society—thus, as it were, it can lie to itself. The result is the disintegration of society and the collapse of a common purpose in a crisis of state whose roots are, however, more internal than external. But the problem can only be remedied when precisely this fact is acknowledged, when causes are not sought outside the state, and external help is not expected.

4. The Special Problem of Intellectual Property

Intellectual property is a particular form of the institutionalization and organization of cultural relationships in modern times. The institution of intellectual property is a regulation in positive law that deals with the rights of exploitation, that is with a surplus-value levy on forms of creativity that are easily reproduced. However, like language and knowledge, easily reproduced forms of creativity belong naturally to the commons of collective ownership and not to the area of exclusive rights of usage of things that are not easily reproduced or "rare" items which form the basis of the legal regimes of property and ownership regarding land and objects.

Thus the battle for "open access" is always a battle against disproportionate and surplus-value levies as imposed by collecting societies on the one hand for example, and "fair" compensation for the work of the creators and authors on the other.

What a good system of rights of usage regarding intellectual (that is easily copyable) products should look like in the age of mechanical reproduction (to use Walter Benjamin's phrase) is much too broad a theme for us to deal with here. It addresses the question of what possibilities of reproduction should remain free, what is to be designated as pirating, and how copyright can be sanctioned in a sufficiently effective way after it is clear that it will be used in the first place, and what it will be used for. In the end the Pirate Party is just a fashionable movement championing a new system of commons with regard to easily reproduced goods.

5. Summary

There are three important points here:

1. Collective law-breaking can be necessary for the development of human rights, for example in the struggle against outdated laws regarding sexuality and marriage. (This contrasts particularly with Convoco's theme this year).
2. Collective law-breaking can constitute threats to a (free, democratic) social order and division of labor in both state and the economy, for example in any kind of Mafia-style nepotism or the collective practice of tax evasion.

3. There are ambivalent cases, for example in the still unresolved dispute about the protection of intellectual property, that is about commons (free availability) in knowledge and other easily reproduced forms.

Notes

1. Thomas Hobbes, *Leviathan* (Oxford: Oxford University Press, 2008).

2. G.W.F. Hegel, *Outlines of the Philosophy of Right* (Oxford: Oxford University Press, 2008).

3. Since 2007 various tax authorities in Germany have bought CDs of illicitly acquired bank information, which provide them with information on individual and institutional cases of tax evasion. This practice is ongoing, and still controversial in Germany. [Translator's note.]

4. On this concept and its problem, cf. in particular Prof. Dr. jur. B. Boemke, Dr. jur. K. Grau, Dipl. Soz. K. Kißling, and Prof. Dr. jur. H. Schneider, "Evidenzbasierte Kriminalprävention im Unternehmen. Wirksamkeit von Compliance-Maßnahmen in der deutschen Wirtschaft – Ein empirisches Forschungsvorhaben," in Pirmin Stekeler-Weithofer (ed.), *Denkströme* 9 (Leipziger Universitätsverlage, 2012); available online at www.denkstroeme. de

5. Cf. the German company Lufthansa AG, http://investor-relations.lufthansa.com/corporate-governance/compliance. html; Hugo Boss, http://annualreport.hugoboss.com/de/glossar. html; or in various management consultancy documents such as Project Consult, http://www.project-consult.de/ecm/wissen/ themen/grc, etc. On "criminal compliance" cf. Thomas Rotsch in Hans Achenbach and Andreas Ransiek (eds.), Handbuch Wirtschaftsstrafrecht, 2nd edn. (Heidelberg, 2011), pp. 45–78, esp. pp. 48 f. (as quoted by Boemke, inter alia, see above).

6. *Corporate Compliance Zeitschrift. Zeitschrift zur Haftungsvermeidung im Unternehmen* [CCZ] has been published since 2008 by C. H. Beck Verlag, and *Risk, Fraud & Compliance.*

Prävention und Aufdeckung in der Compliance-Organisation [ZRFC] has been published since 2006 by Erich Schmidt Verlag (as quoted by Boemke, inter alia, see above).

7. Niklas Luhmann, *Trust and Power* (Chichester: Wiley, 1979).

CHRISTOPH G. PAULUS
REFLECTIONS ON THE LAW IN LIGHT OF COLLECTIVE LAW-BREAKING

I. Examples of collective law-breaking are not just a product of recent times. Even if it seems as if phenomena such as the demonstrations against the Stuttgart 21 project or the financial aid to Greece (undertaken on a bilateral basis in order not to contravene the European, and thus collective, bail-out prohibition of Art. 125 of the TFEU [Treaty on the Functioning of the European Union]) are a totally new development in legal understanding in our states that are founded on the rule of law, the philosopher Seneca (*De beneficiis* III.16.1), for example, teaches us otherwise. He attacks the disadvantage of a legal regulation (his actual example treats a law discussed during the time of Emperor Nero that proposed to make the ingratitude of freed slaves actionable) wherein the frequency of the crime could be made known through the pronouncement of sanctions, thus appeasing the conscience of each individual actual and potential perpetrator. In other words: the larger the number of perpetrators the more lacking in scruples the individual becomes. If everyone evades taxes or makes cellphone calls while driving, we can all feel exonerated.

The fact that it has been around for many years makes the matter under discussion on the one hand easier, but on the other more difficult: easier, because we are thus not limited to the present in our search for causes; more difficult, because this is clearly a basic anthropological phenomenon. When dealing with such basic phenomena we always run the risk of losing ourselves in vagaries and guesswork that lack checkable verification (or falsification). In order to guard against such things, the following thoughts and considerations will be limited to the idea already announced in the title of this essay. It does not claim to offer comprehensive knowledge, but merely an intellectual point of view and a detached reflection on the tension between the law and examples of collective law-breaking.

II. Let us begin by asking the question, what is the law, and what does the law want? Of course asking this question means an immediate supposition that we are dealing with one of the fundamental questions in the theory and philosophy of law. As this is indeed the case and, consequently, as we cannot even begin to reflect on this question which began with Plato and Aristotle at the latest, or only in the broadest strokes, we must content ourselves once again with individual components of the question.

Among these, there is the fact that the law is clearly an inalienable desideratum of human society. This is not only because so-called legal anthropology, with its research into preliterate cultures in particular, suggests this. Rather, we are also today witnessing the attempt (an attempt which has partly already failed, and is partly in the process of failing) to preserve an interpersonal space outside the scope of the law. We are talking about the Internet, with its different platforms and its many areas where, as for example in "Second Life", entire worlds exist in which countless thousands of people cavort about in the guise of their alter ego, or "avatar." However, what immediately becomes clear is that even in such artificial worlds rules are needed to keep community life on the straight and narrow. Although, now as before, a somewhat bitter battle is being fought over the creation, preservation, and maintenance of these Internet areas and societies as law-free spaces, meanwhile, in the courts of our "first life," cases are brought on property rights issues in these artificial worlds, as well as on personality rights or on potentially criminal conduct.

This insight from the most modern of developments recalls ancient Roman wills in which testators ordained that in the case of disputes arising between the heirs the jurists should be kept out (*iurisconsulti abesto*); we know about such clauses because they are discussed in the digests of jurists' collected writings, where jurists report on the different cases they have ruled on in their own legal practices. These jurists, not without a subtle sense of irony, try to arrive at a juristically neat solution without commenting on the failure of the attempt to maintain areas outside the scope of the law.

Consequently there is good evidence that human society craves order and regulation. From the moment Robinson Crusoe and Friday begin to live together, they need manifestly determined rules. If this is indeed the case, we have already reached an early form of law at least, albeit surely not the law itself. For it is clear that simple rules are not yet equivalent to the law: after all we would dispute whether the mechanisms and sanctions operated by the Mafia are for them some kind of legal norms. In order to make the leap into the notion of law, state and constitutional participation in the creation of the rules must clearly be added to the acceptance of the regulation.

Once again these considerations reduce a literally thousand-year-old debate between philosophers, jurists, politicians, and those officiating and acting in the public sphere to an extremely simplified common denominator. This does not make these considerations in themselves wrong, but this representation brings with it a certain shapelessness that can seen as a parallel to the problem of the "Portuguese map" (see J.L. Borges, *Hacedor*). In any case, however, it is clear that state law seems an essential regulatory mechanism for an orderly co-existence within a body politic.

III. Consequently, if the law has an indisputable quasi-anthropological and sociological justification for existing, this insight tells us nothing about what these laws must or should look like. Of course the experience of legal history teaches us that a specific law may not stray too far from what is socially acceptable if it wants to be widely observed. To put it in a somewhat banal way, the legislative content must operate roughly speaking in a more or less wide spectrum of that which normal common sense would regard as legislative content.

In this, of course, there are enormous variations that on the one hand result from the diversity of various societies in various regions of the world; on the other hand, however, they come about from one and the same jurisdiction that the legislator wants to exert behavioral control in an interventionist way over those to whom the law is addressed. Recent examples of the latter situation show success in the case of a smoking ban in restaurants; less so, on the other hand, in prohibiting cellphone use while driving; and none at all in an overly one-sided adjudication of a divorce settlement. Whether such a request for guidance, as for example in the case of the financial crisis where banking regulation is required in many areas, can succeed, we cannot say at present. However the violent opposition of those potentially affected is proof at least of a fear of efficiency.

This orientation towards social acceptance recalls a milestone dispute of 1814 in the development of German law and the law of a unified Germany between the Heidelberg Professor of Law Anton Friedrich Justus Thibaut and his colleague Friedrich Carl von Savigny of the University of Berlin about the need for a general civil law in Germany. While Thibaut considered it desirable and essential for the emerging nation of Germany early on (that is in 1814) to draw up and adopt a unified civil code for the German states (in this, of course, he had in mind the coveted, identity-creating effect of the French *code civil* [or *code Napoléon*] which had been enacted just a few years previously), von Savigny disagreed with him by means of a classic polemical pamphlet titled *Vom Beruf unserer Zeit für Gesetzgebung und Rechtswissenschaft* [Of the Vocation of Our Age for Legislation and Jurisprudence]. This text represented, as it were, the beginning of the German Historical School of Law, which over the decades that followed would make a lasting impression on Germany's legal system. The Historical School championed von Savigny's idea that the law must develop from the people themselves. Even if by that he did not mean a survey of the woman or man on the street, for example but, quite the opposite, a task entrusted to the study of law and thus a highly intellectual one, this does express something of the level of social acceptance we mentioned before.

IV. If, according to the previously mentioned state-created regulatory framework, the law is something that should reasonably orientate itself towards social conditions and particularities, this implies an understanding of the substance of the law that says that the law should be observed just because it is the law. Such an understanding is also an indirect result of the above quote by Seneca according to which the fewer times a legal imperative is infringed, the more efficient the law is. Thus it is a question of an old, reliable concept: the law is to be observed because it is the law. The entire modern concept of the state and of states resides in this premise, and the functioning of social coexistence is based on it.

This sounds more banal than it turns out to be from today's viewpoint. Indeed it is extremely alarming that there are increasing indicators showing a gulf opening up between law-making and observance of the law. To the extent that this occurs, the law is degenerating into arbitrariness, and for the jurists, the foundation of their activity is being pulled away like a carpet from beneath their feet. In this context Stefan Korioth writes appropriately about "symbolic legislation." Even if we set aside all the "high-profile" statements and actions (that is to say those that achieve unfortunate publicity thanks to media attention) of many politicians (from a number of German ministers via Berlusconi to George W. Bush), which in part obscure the law, in part make a mockery of it, even then there remains more than a little evidence for this problem that in business not that many years ago a concept or rather a position has been established which operates under the concept of "compliance" or rather "compliance officer."

The job of this officer, along with his staff that has grown considerably in size in large companies, consists of monitoring and ensuring the observance of regulations. If this were a question of foreign regulations, such as investment protection law in Peru or New Caledonia, it might be understandable and perhaps even appropriate to give someone the job of getting to grips with these and any other foreign laws. However, the compliance department is also responsible for monitoring the observance of domestic laws. It is disconcerting that this is no longer the primary task of the legal department. Compliance has been hived off from it. Clearly this has to do with a number of factors, one of which is surely the enormous mass of regulations which no one can realistically monitor any more, and which grows almost weekly, thus turning the mass of rules we already have into a bottomless pit. Another factor is that the state is clearly and effectively withdrawing more and more from its role of monitoring legal supervision, and is handing over this task to competitors or rivals for example, who can, must, or should ensure the observance of the rules through injunctions or even claims for damages.

If we extrapolate this development and consider its possible implications, then phenomena such as the protests against Stuttgart 12 or Schönefeld airport, or the ever-growing number of citizens' revolts against projects which have already ended up in a legal procedure (a procedure that explicitly provides for the participation of citizens!) appear to be an inevitable consequence. For if this legal procedure itself is no longer synonymous (or even identical) with its binding observance, then the controlling function of the law loses not only its power of persuasion, but also the individual citizen (whether consciously or unconsciously remains to be seen) is separated from regulatory law and from that which one perceives to be the law. The more one's associates share the same idea of the law the more one feels persuaded of "the law". Which brings us back, once again, to Seneca.

INGOLF PERNICE

THE FINANCIAL CRISIS AS THE RESULT— OR THE SUBJECT— OF COLLECTIVE LAW-BREAKING

Introduction

If you type "collective law-breaking" into Google, you will find, among a total of over 10,000 entries, a considerable number of references to the Euro crisis. You will find the accusation, made by FDP Bundestag member Frank Schäffler in particular, that the purchase of Spanish and Italian government bonds by the European Central Bank was an example of collective law-breaking.[1] This is what he said on June 30, 2012 in the debate on the ratification of the European Stability Mechanism Treaty, the Fiscal Pact, and the minor change to the Treaty on the Functioning of the European Union:

> The agreements between European heads of state and of government [are] an engagement in favor of collective law-breaking, which renders null and void the relationship between responsibility and decision-making. The European economic constitution based on freedom as laid out in the Rome Treaties glides step by step over this planned breach of the law in a system of collective irresponsibility that is capable of destroying the unity of Europe.

Thus "the fuse is lit under the house of Europe."

All of which leads us to the central theme of this essay: is the financial crisis the result or the subject of collective law-breaking? Whatever the case the concept of collective law-breaking itself requires a preliminary explanation (I.). We need to ask in particular whether an example of collective law-breaking is to be assessed in law differently from other forms of law-breaking, and whether other political implications emerge in the case of collective law-breaking (II.). Once we have clarified these questions, it will be possible to include the measures for tackling the Euro crisis within them, before we draw our final conclusions.

I. The Concept of Collective Law-Breaking and its Meaning in Law

So what is "collective law-breaking?" The concept is ambiguous, and we can conceive of various different definitions. In this essay, however, what we mean by the term collective law-breaking is the collective refusal to observe the law. It is the claim to an alleged "freedom" which questions the law and its application to the parties concerned; it is a self-empowered disengagement from existing legislation. If norms, to use Niklas Luhmann's terminology, are counterfactual stabilized behavioral expectations,[2] collective law-breaking means a situation where factual behavior opposes the kind of behavior that is expected under the rule of law. The rule of law is not (or no longer) taken seriously, and there is a kind of tacit conspiracy against the law in question. If other people break the law, the perpetrator feels a solidarity with those who also pay less heed to the law—parking offenders, tailgaters on the freeway, those working illegally, environmental polluters, tax evaders, and corrupt individuals. He knows that in many cases the capacity, or even the willingness of the state to apply the rule of law is in his experience small. Here is a topical example: the mass infringement of copyright through video file-sharing or the illegal downloading of music from the Internet, for instance. This is a collective breach of (particularly) national law. But there is more going on here: factual behavior can become a completely new social norm here, and grounds for the search for new national law, a cause taken up by The Pirate Party for example.[3] Law-breaking thus becomes the catalyst for and the basis of a political program.

Does this social, and sometimes political dimension of collective law-breaking have any significance for the legal analysis of law-breaking? No. From the actual circumstances of compliance with the law—what is—we can deduce nothing about the law's claims to validity—what should be. For the legal analysis of law-breaking, it is irrelevant whether it happens as an isolated case or at a mass level through perpetrators acting "in parallel" (as, for example, the thousands of robberies that take place in Germany each year), or by means of an (at least notionally) agreed and thus collective action (see section II.). However, according to this legally positivistic understanding, even an instance of collective law-breaking can change social behavior and even possibly social norms, but it cannot change the law (whether national, supra-national, or international).

Does this understanding not wrongly restrict the notion of people's "freedom"? In answering this I would like to set aside for the moment the aspect of people that is subsumed within a political community—even in borderline cases a collective is after all only one section of all citizens. There is a much more crucial question: is the empowerment that leads to "freedom" from the law a threat to liberty? As a lawyer, and in particular as a constitutional lawyer, I tend to the view that freedom without a legal system cannot be real; it results in chaos and enforcement (not the law) carried out by the stronger elements in society. The law is based on the assurance that everyone can prosper within set limits, and that others, including the state and the EU, respect everyone's legally guaranteed freedoms. Only in this way is peaceful coexistence possible within the state, both in Europe and internationally. Law-breaking threatens the basis of mutual agreement under the law and thus the system of freedom.

II. The Role of the "Collective" in Law-Breaking—the Political Implications

If even one instance of collective law-breaking, seen from the legally positivistic point of view described above, does not create a legal problem, it is certainly not politically insignificant. In this context the will to shape society, as expressed through collective law-breaking, can be conceptualized. To do this we must first define the characteristics of the collective when engaged in collective law-breaking (as we have cited examples of above but not developed further), before we can draw political conclusions on this basis.

First, then: is this mass law-breaking, is any breach of the law committed by many people, an instance of "collective" law-breaking? This seems too far off the mark.

We cannot identify the many individual instances of theft committed each year as collective law-breaking. We might judge the behavior of some of the world's major banks who manipulated the Libor by falsely reporting their interest rates and could have damaged borrowers all over the world in the same way.[4]

Thus the mere parallel behavior of several or many people breaking the law is not enough. The fact that the same offence is committed by many people does not yet turn the deed or deeds into collective law-breaking. But what happens when a breach of the law becomes a (political) movement?

For the breach of the law to be considered "collective," is it necessary for there to exist a commonality of purpose, an albeit hypothetical agreement, or a conscious cooperation between more than one person towards a certain goal? In this case the instances mentioned above of illegal workers and environmental polluters etc., just as much as the case of tax evasion on mass scale, are not relevant: "Super-rich hide more and more money" was the headline in the *Tagesspiegel* of July 23, 2012, "Up to 32 billion dollars shifted into tax havens."[5] Where it is a case of parallel behavior with no attempt at agreement, coordination, or the creation of a movement, we should not describe this as collective law-breaking.

In such a case a critical attitude towards existing legislation is absent. The clients of tax havens are not aiming to generalize their "norm"; they do not want a generalized exemption from paying taxes. For otherwise the state could not provide the services that even this group of people cannot do without. And every individual perpetrator understands this. Rather, their behavior is based on the assumption that existing legislation should be applied to and enforced upon all other taxpayers. The fact that all of them commit the same breach of the law does not turn them into a collective.

So what then makes the collective into a collective? Agreement, or in any case a common goal and coordinated action, should be the criteria. In this respect organized crime just as much as the illegal business cartel would be examples of collective law-breaking. Joint action in this case is not oriented towards an actual or alleged "counter-norm" or even "counter-conduct"[6] against existing legislation, but it is a simple, possibly criminal infringement of the law. But this in itself may not be sufficient.

Both criteria, that of commonality of purpose and alleged counter-norm, could however be fulfilled by the coordinated action taken nevertheless against international law by the "coalition of the willing" in the case of the war in Kosovo, or Iraq which went ahead without a mandate from the UN Security Council.[7] This then would be a case of collective law-breaking. The specious attempt at justification by means of a photo, which apparently pointed to the existence of weapons of mass destruction, does not in this case indicate counter-conduct, or a counter-norm. However the new legal principle of humanitarian intervention or the "responsibility to protect"[8] might be the intended counter-norm. With regard to the still valid fundamental principle of the sovereign equality of all nations (Art. 2, section 1 of the UN Charter) and the prohibition of violence and intervention (Art. 2, section 4, UNC), this new principle would be tantamount to an acknowledgment of a partial revolution taking place in international law.

Another instance is the refusal to implement EU directives by a number of Member States, if they can derive a questionable political and economic advantage by so doing. This is a breach of the law, but lacks the notion of the "collective" in the sense we have discussed. Does this also apply to the Data Retention Directive?[9] Germany is failing to discharge its obligations regarding EU law if, long after the expiry of the implementation period, it consciously does not bring German law in line with the Data Retention Directive.[10] The liberal idea behind this directive is the protection of personal data and thus of the right to informational self-determination. Even if this is not infringed through the requirements of the directive in a way that triggers judicial control,[11] this refusal to implement does aim to avoid endangering the German Constitution, and thus aims at more freedom. The "counter-norm," the freedom from the duty to implement six-monthly data storage, thus becomes conceivable, and a change to the directive is already being debated.[12] Classifying this refusal as collective law-breaking would however probably be difficult due to a lack of any kind of "perceived" community, even if other Member States follow Germany's lead for similar reasons. Each is acting on their own behalf. Ultimately the criterion of "collectivity" is not fulfilled because the government's non-action is carried out in the name of the "collective" German people—or because it corresponds to the will of a political party? This would indeed be taking things too far.

Consequently we can see that two criteria must be fulfilled if are to talk about collective law-breaking: first, we need a certain degree of community between several law-breakers, or at any rate a feeling of community that will distinguish collective law-breaking from mere parallel behavior, even if this behavior takes place at a mass level. Second, the notion of a counter-norm (albeit in no way established or generally accepted) appears to play a role, and the action of law-breaking could, however, result in the recognition of this counter-norm over the course of time.

Now what does it mean to have defined collective law-breaking? As we have already discussed, collective law-breaking has no meaning in law, but it does have a social and thus a political meaning. As we have seen in the context of the Pirate Party, the grouping of social ideas in concert with a counter-norm can easily become a political tool. In this respect there is a program of changing the law that lies at the heart of the counter-norm—and this distinguishes the effect of an appeal through collective law-breaking from those breaches of the law that are not aiming to change the legal situation.

A second aspect of political skill, in instances of collective law-breaking in any case, is that of effective law enforcement. Once again let's look at this through an example: the desire to manage the crisis incurred by breaches of copyright law through warnings, penalties, and coercion has proved to have little effect. The uploading and downloading of copyrighted works or file-sharing through international online networks for music, movies, and computer games cannot be suppressed simply through "command and control" regulation. A change in the law that is acceptable to all interested parties is proving difficult and is not in prospect. So in the first instance there remains perhaps only a third solution, which changes the way in which laws are implemented. Copyright law must be understood in light of the social realities and social norms that Mark F. Schultz calls "copy norms"; they must be communicated to users, thus helping to make the legitimacy of copyright acceptable and even ultimately implementing it without recourse to sanctions.[13]

III. Collective Law-Breaking and the Euro

What, then, is going on in the case of the collective action of governments in their attempt to rescue the Euro, as denounced by Frank Schäffler?

This is surely an instance when the criterion of "collectivity" has been fulfilled; one could even say this is an example of "cooperative" action. This is specific to international law, as it is not the EU acting as a legal entity in "supranational" mode, but rather state governments. In the bailout program no competences are transferred to the EU; there is no centralization of power, as would only be possible under Article 23, section 1 of the German Constitution.

In the agreements on rescuing the Euro Member States act cooperatively through international law, precisely because this does not come under European jurisdiction, and the necessary transfer of economic and fiscal competences to the EU through treaty changes seemed politically pointless. If it were a question of currency policy in the narrower sense, for which the EU is exclusively responsible (see Article 3, section 1, clause (c), TFEU) there would be fewer problems. But since this affects the economic and fiscal policy of Member States, an area where the States have retained their powers, they are also permitted to establish mutual obligations based on international law.

There remains the question of whether the rescue provisions (including new agreements such as the European Stability Mechanism, minor treaty changes, and the Fiscal Pact) contain a breach of the law, and if so, why. In the literature on this subject the question is extremely controversial, and was even brought before the German Federal Constitutional Court in the form of an urgent application against the ratification of the treaties in question. Here, in a judgment of September 12, 2012, the Court ruled that in the interpretation of EU law a violation of the ban on providing overdraft facilities according to Article 123 of the TFEU cannot be determined "as an essential element in the safeguarding of the German constitutional requirements of the democratic principle according to EU law."[14] So my response to this question is no. This is not a breach in the law (see point 1 below), but rather law-breaking is to be found in the run-up to this, that is in the repeated disregard of obligations which the Member States imposed upon themselves in the Maastricht Treaty on the conception and setting-up of the economic and monetary union itself (see point 2 below). Perhaps a possible further breach of the law, namely the reckless capital spending policy of the banking sector, also set everything in train (see point 3 below).

1. Are the Euro Rescue Packages a Breach of the Law?

At the heart of the criticism brought before the German Constitutional Court is the charge that Germany is committing itself financially way into the future beyond its budgetary resources, and thus the budgetary autonomy of the German Bundestag, which is central to a healthy democracy, would be unduly restricted.[15] The Court did not accept this in the proceedings about the bailout, and now too in the summary proceedings against the ratification of the ESM and the Fiscal Pact the Court has rejected the application with the proviso that the limitation of liability under the Treaty according to Article 8 of the Treaty establishing the ESM is ensured against any doubt by a corresponding explanation in the context of ratification.[16] The Court considers that the judgment as to whether Germany's payment obligations as agreed under the ESM might not lead "to a complete drain on budgetary autonomy" should be made by the legislature.[17] So long as the agreements do not incur an "automatic guarantee or performance… whose effects are not limited", an infringement of the principle of democracy, even according to the earlier judgment, does not take place even if the obligations grow to a extent, which "by reason of their scale may be of structural significance for parliament's right to decide on the budget, for example by giving guarantees the honoring of which may endanger budget autonomy." In this case, however, the Court demands that any dealings with the available means be subject to parliamentary oversight.[18] As the Court has now established in respect to the Treaty establishing the ESM, even the regulations on immunity and confidentiality in this Treaty are compatible with the German Constitution, if it is guaranteed by means of appropriate explanations that sufficient parliamentary oversight of the ESM is possible via the German Bundestag.[19]

The fact that within the framework of the ESM and the Fiscal Pact, institutions of the EU, in particular the European Commission and the Court of Justice, can be tasked with particular jobs without any special provisions being incorporated into the Treaties,[20] is however not a constitutional problem because of the ratification of the Treaties according to Article 23, paragraph 1, sentence 1 of the German Constitution. It is only called into question under Article 13, paragraph 2 of the Treaty on European Union. According to this, if each institution "shall act within the limits of the powers conferred on it in the Treaties," the demands, for example of the European Commission on the basis of an agreement under international law, does not correspond to EU law, even if it is merely a question of "borrowed administration."

While this irregularity in public affairs is given no further attention, the attacks on the Euro bailout policy are primarily directed at their compatibility with the bans on the issuing of credit facilities and the purchase of government bonds on the primary market (Article 123, paragraph 1, TFEU) on the one hand, and with the bailout ban of Article 125, paragraph 1 of the

TFEU on the other.[21] Is this a breach of the law? Both proscriptions are a consequence of Member States being responsible for their own budgetary policy—and for the consequences of their possibly unsound budgetary policy. According to EU law no Member State—nor any creditor of a Member State— should be able to count on resorting to central banks or even the liability or the intervention of other Member States in the case of financial problems. The restraints resulting from this should act as a disciplining force on the economic and financial policy of the Member States.

However, Articles 123 and 125 of the TFEU do not prohibit the central banks, in particular the ECB, from acquiring government bonds on the secondary market, that is from the banks. Usually the ECB accepts this kind of securities in return for injecting banks with fresh funds with which the banks in turn supply the market with money at the appropriate rate of interest after making due checks on each debtor on a case-by-case basis. The ECB acquired such debt securities in May 2010 in light of the danger that the bond market might come to a complete standstill—even in interbank lending—in the context of its "Securities Markets Programme,"[22] buying them at current market value, that is not at their face value. That could entail price reductions of up to 40% and more. If the interest rate is calculated according to the face value, the interest accruing to the ECB, measured in terms of the capital invested, is correspondingly higher.

One might argue that this was working counter to the disciplining aim of Article 123 of the TFEU. However, before we allege avoidance or even breach of the law, we should test whether in the given situation the objective "to address the malfunctioning of securities markets and restore an appropriate monetary policy transmission mechanism"[23] does not correspond to the original remit of the European Central Bank. So long as the ECB and the national central banks do not directly buy bonds from Member States the definition of the ban outlined in Article 123 of the TFEU, at least according to the letter of the law, is not fulfilled. But even the purpose of the regulation is not undermined, for the pressure on the crisis states is maintained. This is not a breach of the law.

Even Article 125 of the TFEU is not infringed. That the granting of interest-bearing loans is not a bailout, may not convince those who invoke the "private investor test," well-known from laws on state aid, and who maintain that under current circumstances no private bank would issue any more loans to Greece, nor latterly to Ireland, Portugal, and Spain. However, crucial for this interpretation is what exactly is excluded in the regulations, what is the letter of the law, then what is the context of the regulations in the general scheme of the chapter in the Treaty, and finally what is its purpose. According to the letter of the Treaty, Article 125 of the TFEU precludes the ECB or another Member State from being liable for or intervening on behalf of another Member State's debts. That means that a creditor can have recourse neither to the ECB nor to a Member State if another Member State does not pays its debts. That the ECB cannot give the debtor state any credit follows explicitly from Article 123, paragraph 1, sentence 1 of the TFEU. Nowhere, however, does it state that this would be forbidden to other Member States. Thus from this general scheme it also follows that loans between the Member States—or guarantees of loans—are also not proscribed even in the case of imminent financial difficulties.

Against this we could once again invoke the aim of a disciplining function. It is an important argument, for without budgetary discipline as outlined in the Treaty the monetary union cannot function in each Euro country. In a situation where, after the bankruptcy of a Member State, other faltering states might also collapse as if in a domino effect, and as a result the entire structure might threaten to collapse, it is difficult to give priority to the aim of discipline above that of rescuing the Euro as a whole. In any case this teleological argument does not permit the interpretation of the clause of Article 125 of the TFEU beyond the letter of the clause as a proscription of loans between Member States, if such an action would exclude the protection of the currency itself. For this reason Greece's bailout package was not, and the agreements on the temporary bailout offered by the EFSM and the ESFS which propped up Ireland and Portugal are not a breach of the law and consequently also not an example of collective law-breaking.

Through this "small" amendment to the Treaty (Article 136 III TFEU) any lingering doubts about the compatibility of these compromises and of the ESM with the bailout ban in Article 125 of the TFEU are dispelled. For the amendment clearly states that "Member States whose currency is the Euro may establish a stability mechanism to be activated if indispensable to safeguard the stability of the Euro area as a whole." The fundamental aim of stability for preserving the Euro is emphasized in that "the granting of any required financial assistance under the mechanism [must] be made subject to strict conditionality." In this way Member States are officially informed that they are not prevented from taking measures if, because of the crisis in a Member State for example in the face of expected contagion effects, the Euro as a whole is in danger and intervention—financially and in light of the constraints—appears essential.

2. The Financial Crisis: The Result of Collective Law-Breaking in the EU?

In view of this we must look for collective law-breaking elsewhere. It is the disregard of obligations that the governments of the Member States adopted through the Maastricht Treaty in order to guarantee the functionality of the common currency. The results were predictable and were warned about in advance.[24]

The "European economic constitution based on freedom as laid out in the Rome Treaties" that Frank Schäffler describes is the system of European treaties that have constituted and organized the internal market, and have also created a common currency for this market. This system is a community based on the rule of law, as Walter Hallstein said, "it is created by law, it is a source of the law, and it is the system of law."[25] On this we base the trust that sustains our coexistence without violence and coercion. The importance of the law and its observance has not been expressed better than by Paul Kirchhof in his recent FAZ article: "The EU is in crisis because the law was disregarded."[26] And the financial crisis in Europe is surely the clearest example of the devastating consequences that collective law-breaking can have—for the European economic constitution based on freedom and thus for the living conditions of the citizens of Europe that are also based on freedom. We are talking about such things as:

• the politically motivated agreement to admit Greece into the Eurozone in full knowledge that she did not fulfill the Maastricht criteria;

• the manipulation of balance sheets reporting Greece's position, and also Germany's resistance to checking such reports through the EU;

• the unprecedented violation of stability criteria by Germany and France and the avoidance of any penalties imposed by the Council of the EU.

These are examples of collective law-breaking. Since the Eurozone governments have not taken seriously their obligations both to Treaties and to secondary legislation in coordinating and disciplining the economic and fiscal policies for which they were responsible, the economic and monetary union has entered a crisis whose solution is by no means certain.[27] The responsibility for this is borne by all the Member States; they are caught up in the disregard of their own system. The "counter-norm" is not easily identifiable. It may lie in a somewhat more flexible practice of managing common rules, in the tacit agreement that the law operates as a "soft law," and that these are "only" contractual obligations from which one can deviate without incurring sanctions.

Thus it is not in itself the constitutional asymmetry of a cooperative economic union and a centralized monetary union that led to the crisis.[28] The edifice of Maastricht would not have had to break down if the Member States had honored the trust in compliance with the rule of law that they had set for themselves— and if the financial markets, faced with infringements, had reacted as had been accepted, namely by punishing unsound Member States immediately through a hike in interest rates.

But the banks did not react as they were supposed to. According to their self-selected strategy, their own advantage was more important to them than the punishment of unsound governments.[29] The fact that politicians made an error of judgment in appointing the banks as guardians of budgetary discipline within the system may have been a mistake on the part of the architects of the Euro. But the infringement of budgetary discipline, that is to say, the breach of the law, is the responsibility of the Member States alone.

3. Lehman Brothers and the Crisis in America

Perhaps another cause of the EU crisis was the case of Lehman Brothers and the American crisis—possibly another example of collective law-breaking. Anyone who systematically bundles high-risk mortgage loans into so-called "securities" and offers them on the international finances markets re-packaged again and again with other products, and presented as a particularly safe investment, will find it hard to escape the allegation of fraud. And, during this, the rating agencies' practice of handing out spurious top marks increases the suspicion of deliberate collusion. It was predictable that the system is fragile and thus high risk.[30] Early on experts had warned of the slump in the US property market and the possible collapse of the international finance market.[31] Clearly people did not want to recognize this. Quick profits and big bonuses seduced people into violating their duties of care and due diligence at all levels. In their concluding remarks on March 10, 2011 the Financial Crisis Inquiry Commission stated:

> We conclude this financial crisis was avoidable. The crisis was the result of human action and inaction, not of Mother Nature or computer models gone haywire. The captains of finance and the public stewards of

our financial system ignored warnings and failed to question, understand, and manage evolving risks within a system essential to the well-being of the American public. Theirs was a big miss, not a stumble. While the business cycle cannot be repealed, a crisis of this magnitude need not have occurred. To paraphrase Shakespeare, the fault lies not in the stars, but in us.[32]

We know what happened next, both in Germany and in Europe as a whole.

Conclusion

There are those who see a connection between the crisis in Europe and the pressure that resulted from the international crisis. Speculation about the causes is a matter for economists and historians. What we need today are two things that are closely connected:

• the immediate abolition of structural weaknesses in the Economic and Monetary Union (EMU), namely the asymmetry of its construction. This is a prerequisite for its functionality, for the guarantee of monetary stability, and thus of assets in the economic and monetary union;

• regulation of the financial markets so that politics is not at the mercy of the whims of the markets, but rather a legal framework is constructed for the markets, in which the democratically determined common good is not marginalized.[33]

The law cannot protect us from collective law-breaking, and similarly it cannot protect us from crises that it may itself create. However, defending the regulating effect of the law and its observance, until the perhaps necessary changes in constitutionally established procedures have been decided and implemented, should be the task of everyone. For the law is the condition of freedom, just as a functional economic and monetary union is a prerequisite for the protection of assets in Europe.

This essay is based on the lecture given by Prof. Dr. Ingolf Pernice at the Convoco Forum on July 28, 2012 in Salzburg. The discussion of the judgment of the German Constitutional Court of September 12, 2012, which was, at the time of the lecture, still pending, has been updated to reflect the current situation.

Notes

1. *ECB Bond Purchase—Collective Law-Breaking*. Kopp-Nachrichten news item with Roland Lieber, August 9, 2011.

2. Niklas Luhmann, *A Sociological Theory of Law*, trans. Elizabeth King and Martin Albrow (London: Routledge & Kegan Paul, 1985), p. 63.

3. Cf. The Pirate Party on copyright law, http://www.piratenpartei. de/politik/wissensgesellschaft/urheberrecht/ (accessed August 19, 2012).

4. Cf. "Banken. 'Schäbiger Umgang'. Ein Skandal um manipulierte Zinssätze erschüttert Europas Finanzbranche," in *Der Spiegel* 28, 2012, pp. 64 ff.

5. Albert Funk, "*32 Billionen Dollar in Steueroasen*. Studie: Superreiche verstecken immer mehr Geld," in *Der Tagesspiegel*,

http://www.tagesspiegel.de/politik/32-billionen-dollar-in-steueroasen-studie-superreiche-verstecken-immer-mehr-geld/6907630.html (accessed August 6, 2012).

6. This draws on Michel Foucault's analytical framework, cf. *Security, Territory, Population: Lectures at the Collège de France, 1977–78*, trans. Graham Burchell (London: Picador, 2009), p. 191.

7. Cf. for example, Eyal Benvenisti, "The US and the Use of Force: Double-edged Hegemony and the Management of Global Emergencies," in *European Journal of International Law [EJIL]* (2004), vol. 15, no. 4, pp. 677, 678. On the debate about breaches of international law cf. for example Michael Bothe, "Terrorism and the Legality of Pre-emptive Force," in *EJIL* (2003), vol. 14, no. 2, pp. 227ff.; William K. Lietzau, "The Role of Military Force in Foreign Relations, Humanitarian Intervention and the Security Council," in *Zeitschrift für ausländisches öffentliches Recht und Völkerrecht [ZaöRV]*, 64 (2004), pp. 281ff; Nico Krisch, "Review Essay: Legality, Morality and the Dilemma of Humanitarian Intervention after Kosovo," in *EJIL* (2002), vol. 13, no. 1, pp. 323 ff.

8. Cf. for example Elis Schmeer, *Responsibility to Protect und Wandel von Souveränität* (Berlin: Berliner Wissenschafts-Verlag, 2010), pp. 1 ff, 28. Gareth Evans and Mohamed Sahnoun, "The Responsibility to Protect," in *Foreign Affairs* (2002), vol. 81, no. 6, pp. 99 ff.; Anne Orford, *International Authority and the Responsibility to Protect* (Cambridge: CUP, 2011).

9. Directive 2006/24/EC of the European Parliament and of The Council of March 15, 2006 on the retention of data generated or processed in connection with the provision of publicly available electronic communications services or of public communications networks, and amending Directive 2002/58/EC in *Official Journal of the European Union*, no. L105 of April 13, 2006, pp. 54–63. http://eur-lex.europa.eu/LexUriServ/LexUriServ.do?uri=OJ:L:2006:105:0054:0063:EN:PDF (accessed August 19, 2012).

10. Cf. "Vorratsdatenspeicherung: Deutschland droht erstmals Millionstrafe," in faz.net, April 21, 2012. http://www.faz.net/aktuell/politik/inland/vorratsdatenspeicherung-deutschland-droht-erstmals-million-strafe-11725523.html (accessed August 6, 2012).

11. According to the German Constitutional Court, 1 BvR 256/08 of March 2, 2010. http://www.bverfg.de/entscheidungen/rs20100302_1bvr025608.html, margin no. 180ff (accessed 8 July, 2012).

12. S. Heise online news of April, 7, 2012: "EU-Kommission: Neue Richtlinie zur Vorratsdatenspeicherung kommt 2013." http://www.heise.de/newsticker/meldung/EU-Kommission-Neue-Richtlinie-zur-Vorratsdatenspeicherung-kommt-2013-1631714.html (accessed August 19, 2012).

13. Mark F. Schultz, *Copynorms: Copyright Law and Social Norms* (2006) in http://ebookbrowse.com/schultz-mark-copynorms-pdf-d40899074, esp. pp. 29 ff (accessed August 6, 2012).

14. On the debate see for example Franz C. Mayer, "Karlsruhe soll nicht ständig Zäune errichten," in *taz*, July 4, 2012, p. 7; see also Quentin Peel "Germany's Judgement Day," in *Financial Times* of August 7, 2012 http://www.ft.com/cms/s/0/78df7420-dfa5-11e1-9bb7-00144feab49a.html#axzz22xOx3PFl (accessed August 8, 2012). See also German Constitutional Court, 2 BvR 1390/12 – ESM margin note 276 ff http://www.bverfg.de/entscheidungen/rs20120912_2bvr139012.html. The Court did not give an opinion on Art. 125 TFEU here. In any event questions on the infringement of EU law, should they prove to be relevant to the issue, would however have to be decided during the main proceedings of the Constitutional Court not without submitting documentation to the European Court of Justice according to Art. 267 TFEU.

15. German Constitutional Court, 2 BvR 1390/12. On the delivery of the judgment on the request for interim measures on September 12, 2012 cf. the press release of July 16, 2012 http://www.bundesverfassungsgericht.de/pressemitteilungen/bvg12-055.html (accessed August 19, 2012).

16. German Constitutional Court, 2 BvR 1390/12 of September 12, 2012 – ESM, introductory sentence 1, and margin note 241 ff, 253 http://www.bverfg.de/entscheidungen/rs20120912_2bvr139012.html.

17. German Constitutional Court, 2 BvR 1390/12 of September 12, 2012 – ESM, margin note 271 http://www.bverfg.de/entscheidungen/rs20120912_2bvr139012.html.

18. German Constitutional Court, 2 BvR 987/10 of September 7, 2011, bailout package, http://www.bverfg.de/entscheidungen/rs20110907_2bvr098710.html (accessed August 8, 2012).

19. German Constitutional Court, 2 BvR 1390/12 of September 12, 2012 – ESM, margin note 254 ff., 280 ff. http://www.bverfg.de/entscheidungen/rs20120912_2bvr139012.html.

20. Cf. for example Art. 3, para. 2 of the Fiscal Pact: "common principles to be proposed by the European Commission" for the corrective mechanism which should guarantee the maintenance of the debt cap; Art. 8, para. 1 of the Fiscal Pact: report by the European Commission on the debt cap and the corrective mechanism and opinion on the fulfillment of duties by the Member State, and the jurisdiction of the Court of Justice (Art. 273 TFEU) all the way to an imposition of a fine or a penalty payment. Correspondingly see Art. 5, para. 6 item (g) of the ESM: "to give a mandate to the European Commission to negotiate, [...], the economic policy conditionality attached to each financial assistance"; Art. 13, para. 1 of the ESM: assessment of the risk and the financing needs of a Member State in the context of stability support; Art. 13, paras. 3 and 4 of the ESM: negotiation and signature of the Memorandum of Understanding; Art. 13 para. 7 of the ESM: monitoring and assignment of monitoring and reporting duties. In Art. 37, para. 3 of the ESM the Court of Justice of the European Union is deemed responsible for the settlement of any disputes, as per Art. 273 of the TFEU.

21. The literature on this topic is vast and includes: Stefan Korioth, "There is No Alternative, or Original Sin? The European States' Rescue Package of May 2010," in Corinne Michaela Flick (ed.), *Can't Pay, Won't Pay? Sovereign Debt and the Challenge of Growth in Europe* (London: Convoco! Editions 2012), pp. 109, 118 ff; with numerous references: Christian Calliess, "Das europäische Solidaritätsprinzip und die Krise des Euro – Von der Rechtsgemeinschaft zur Solidaritätsgemeinschaft?" lecture given at the Forum Constitutionis Europae on January 18, 2011, FCE 01/11, esp. pp. 37 ff http://www.whi-berlin.eu/tl_files/FCE/Rede_Calliess.pdf (accessed August 24, 2012).

22. Decision of the European Central Bank of May 14, 2010 establishing a securities markets program (ECB/2010/5)

(2010/281/EU), *Official Journal of the European Union*, 2010, L124/8.

23. Ibid., third recital.

24. See for example Guy Kirsch, "Die Eurokrise ist (nicht nur) eine Währungskrise," in *Aus Politik und Zeitgeschichte* (2010) no. 43 http://www.bpb.de/apuz/32436/die-euro-krise-ist-nicht-nur-eine-waehrungskrise-essay?p=all (accessed August 19, 2012).

25. Walter Hallstein, *Der unvollendete Bundestaat* (1969), p. 33. For more on the background and detail of Walter Hallstein's concept and on the consequences for the qualification of the EU as a constitutional union see Ingolf Pernice, "Begründung und Konsolidierung der Europäischen Gemeinschaft als Rechtsgemeinschaft," in Manfred Zuleeg (ed.), *Der Beitrag Walter Hallsteins zur Zukunft Europas, Referate zu Ehren von Walter Hallstein*, (Baden-Baden: Nomos, 2003), pp. 56–70, also available as a paper published by the Walter Hallstein Institute, WHI Paper 2009/01 http://www.whi-berlin.eu/whi-paper-2009.html.pdf (accessed August 8 2012).

26. "Paul Kirchhof on the EU crisis. Verfassungsnot!" in *Frankfurter Allgemeine Zeitung*, July 12, 2012 http://www.faz.net/aktuell/feuilleton/debatten/europas-zukunft/paul-kirchhof-zur-krise-der-eu-verfassungsnot-11817188.html (accessed August 8, 2012).

27. Cf. also the critical comments in Kevin Featherstone, "The Maastricht Roots of the Euro Crisis," in *Social Europe Journal*, March 30, 2012, http://www.social-europe.eu/2012/03/the-maastricht-roots-of-the-euro-crisis (accessed August 19, 2012).

28. Accordingly, but in the face of many other opinions, George Soros, Institute for New Economic thinking in Berlin, 2012, http://ineteconomics.org/blog/inet/george-soross-speech-opening-session-inet-berlin.pdf (accessed August 19, 2012), p. 13: "The Maastricht Treaty was fundamentally flawed, demonstrating the fallibility of the authorities. Its main weakness was well known to its architects: it established a monetary union without a political union. The architects believed however, that when the need arose the political will could be generated to take the necessary steps towards a political union."

29. Cf. ibid., p. 16 f.

30. Cf. for example Stephen Mihm, "Dr. Doom," in *New York Times Magazine*, August 15, 2008: "On Sept. 7, 2006, Nouriel Roubini, an economics professor at New York University, stood before an audience of economists at the International Monetary Fund and announced that a crisis was brewing. In the coming months and years, he warned, the United States was likely to face a once-in-a-lifetime housing bust, an oil shock, sharply declining consumer confidence and, ultimately, a deep recession. He laid out a bleak sequence of events: homeowners defaulting on mortgages, trillions of dollars of mortgage-backed securities unraveling worldwide and the global financial system shuddering to a halt. These developments, he went on, could cripple or destroy hedge funds, investment banks and other major financial institutions like Fannie Mae and Freddie Mac" http://www.nytimes.com/2008/08/17/magazine/17pessimist-t.html?_r=3&pagewanted=all (accessed August 19, 2012).

31. For example with reference to Nassim Nicholas Taleb's *The Black Swan*, David Brooks, "The Behavioral Revolution," in *New York Times*, October 27, 2009.

32. Financial Crisis Inquiry Commission, Conclusions of March 10, 2011, http://cybercemetery.unt.edu/archive/fcic/ (accessed August 10, 2012).

33. See discussions of this in Ingolf Pernice, Matthias Wendel, Lars S. Otto, Kristin Bettge, Martin Mlynarski, and Michael Schwarz, *Die Krise demokratisch überwinden. Reformansätze für eine demokratisch fundierte Wirtschafts- und Finanzverfassung Europas/A Democratic Solution for the Crisis. Reform Steps Towards a Democratically Based Economic and Financial Constitution for Europe* (Nomos, 2012).

JÜRGEN STARK
QUO VADIS, EUROPE?

Talking about the crisis in Europe, the future of the economic and monetary union, and the future of European integration means first of all that we must understand the present, and in particular we must be aware of the reasons that have led to this present crisis.

We must ask questions about the political system. And if we are discussing the institutional framework of the economic and monetary union, we cannot ignore the principles and rules that were established by treaty and that form what we might call the "commercial basis" of the economic and monetary union as a community based on stability, and on which a culture of stability is created.

Escalation of the Crisis

At the moment we are in a new stage of escalation in the crisis in Europe. More and more Member States of the Euro area require external financial aid. Necessary economic adjustments threaten to exert too many demands on the democratic systems. Established under strict conditions financial aid to the crisis-hit countries is encountering limitations, whether it be "adjustment fatigue" here, or "bailout fatigue" there. The costs of additional aid to other Member States and the time frame of the economic reforms and fiscal consolidation threaten not only to reduce the effectiveness of firewalls, but also to exert more and more demands on the economic performance of the dwindling number of donor countries. Crisis management becomes more and more expensive—and for how much longer? And what will be the consequences?

In Germany in particular a wide-ranging and lively debate has flared up among economists and lawyers about the way the crisis has been managed. It has focused in particular on the risks incurred and the mid- to long-term effects of short-term political measures on the future, and on the character of the monetary union, as well as the process of European integration. If we remove the emotion from this debate, we can pose three main questions that are closely interlinked:

1. Does Europe need new impetus towards integration? If so, what should this new Europe look like? Will it be a development from a union of states into a federal state? Under what conditions will this take place, and with what consequences? Or is this a return to the "Maastricht consensus"?

2. What is the meaning of a paradigm shift from a community based on stability to a union based on liability and debt, in which Member States are responsible for the debts and risks of other EU countries, increasingly jeopardizing their own creditworthiness? What would the consequences of this be for monetary policy and the value of our currency?

3. How do we define the extent of democratic control? What about the rights of parliament at national level? This also raises the question of the degree of integration: what depth of integration is politically desirable? What is constitutionally possible?

The Maastricht Approach

Through the economic and monetary union we Europeans have reached the highest—and most visible—degree of integration. This is particularly true of the monetary sector. Neither in foreign and security policy, nor in domestic and legal policy is there a comparable degree of uniformity. These policies have remained more or less intergovernmental, despite all attempts to develop community-based elements. The economic and monetary union is without doubt a political project. However it is also the logical outcome of the European process of integration and in particular the culmination in monetary terms of the single market. Of course the idea of monetary integration did not just appear at the end of the 1980s. The EEC Treaty of 1957 already contained statements about monetary and currency policy.

Nevertheless economic and monetary union has remained a "limping construct." On the one hand the economic and monetary union each present a different degree of integration and uniformity. On the other it is a union without "political union" in the sense of increased integration between states. Thus political—

and fiscal—integration have lagged behind monetary integration. Other European partners refused the parallels between monetary union and "political union" promoted by Germany during the negotiations over the Maastricht Treaty (although it was never clearly defined what was to be understood by "political union"). They were not prepared to give up their national sovereignty, for example in the area of foreign and security policy. Neither the Amsterdam Treaty nor the Nice or Lisbon Treaties have changed anything fundamentally in this respect.

Nevertheless with the Maastricht approach to monetary union a solid basis was created consisting of contractually binding principles and rules as well as new procedures and instruments. The crucial drawback was the inadequate implementation and oversight of the new, extremely challenging (and thus fragile) regime of unified fiscal policy for which the European Central Bank is responsible, and of economic policy that has remained to a large extent at national level.

Admittedly the intention was that the economic policy of the Member States would be more closely coordinated (Art. 119–121 of the Treaty). To do this principles for the community's economic policy were developed beginning in 1993/94 with recommendations specific to each country. This kind of "soft" coordination remained largely a bureaucratic exercise. The impact of the principles on national economic policies remained limited, as there was no effective monitoring. The regular reporting on the implementation of recommendations, as stipulated in the Treaty, was wantonly neglected. Here the aim of coordinating economic policy was to attain a lasting economic convergence of Member States and to safeguard this after the third stage of economic and monetary union had been entered into.

The rules concerning individual states' budgets were made more binding, in particular with the concretization and operationalization of the Treaty's provisions (Art. 126), through the Stability and Growth Pact. The Stability Pact had an impact in the first years after the introduction of the Euro. However the first major test of the Pact turned out to be a negative experience. When in 2003 Germany and France reported an excessive deficit almost simultaneously, and the next stage of the procedure should have been introduced with the possibility of imposing penalties later on, both countries refused to acknowledge the consequences as laid down in the Treaty. With this infringement of the terms of the Treaty, the Stability Pact was effectively destroyed. For (short-term) political reasons, no one wanted to accept any directives from Brussels, preferring to maintain an unrestricted sphere of influence over their own fiscal policy, and seeing in such directives a threat to their national sovereignty. But was sovereignty in budgetary questions not already restricted by the ratification of the Maastricht Treaty and the approval of the Stability Pact? Whatever the case, the Pact's rationale of protecting monetary union through fiscal policy rules in the absence of political integration was cast aside.

The subsequent reform of the Pact in 2005 only served to prove the ineffectiveness of the rules.

Another important basis of the economic and monetary union is the "no bailout" clause (Art. 125 of the Treaty). This basis arises from the principle of Member States' responsibility for their own political actions. It provides for the exclusion of liability for the debts of other countries. Proceeding from the assumption that only mature countries qualify for entry into the monetary union and that necessary adjustments must be managed by the countries themselves, the Treaty did not provide for the possibility of financial support in the case of individual countries developing a crisis as a result of membership of the monetary union. In this, one proceeded implicitly from the fact that if a country gets into financial difficulties or even goes bankrupt, the necessary adjustment and, if required, external public financing should take place outside the Euro area.

People were fully aware of the risk that the monetary union could lead to financial transfers. For this reason at Germany's initiative on May 1, 1998, the day of the decision about Member States' qualification for the third stage of economic and monetary union, a resolution was passed by the European finance ministers which explicitly prohibited financial transfers resulting from membership of the monetary union. This resolution was endorsed by heads of state and government at the European Council meeting of June 1998 in Cardiff. When the question became pertinent at a later stage, it was explained that such a political resolution is not legally binding. However it was certainly a political declaration of intent and should at least be regarded as a guideline for interpretation!

For the Euro area, the Maastricht Treaty and the statutes of the European Central Bank and European System of Central Banks created a solid framework for a new European monetary system (Art. 127ff. of the Treaty). The ECB was given a clear mandate to guarantee monetary stability as its central goal. In addition the ECB/ESCB were set up independently of political influence. The degree of independence of the ECB, which is defined in terms of its personnel, institutions, finance, and instrumental role, is formally and legally extremely high. The ECB's mandate and independence reflect the regulatory approach of the primacy of monetary stability as the crucial constituting principle of a functioning system based on a market economy. Equally, the prohibition of monetary financing by states is anchored in the Treaty. In this way both Treaty and statues reflect the paradigm of "monetary dominance" over economic and financial policy.

The rehearsal of these principles—with particular emphasis on budgetary rules, the "no bailout" clause, the independence of the central bank, the primacy of price stability, and the prohibition of monetary financing— shows that "Maastricht" is a solid approach that is unambiguously focused on stability. The argument that this approach has failed is not correct. Rather, what is correct is that the approach was never fully implemented. Or did it in fact "fail" because it was not implemented or was not implementable because it was too complicated and too much of a challenge for too many Member States? Was too much expected of the Member States, and were these standards not fulfilled because of that? It should be clear that the above principles and rules are indispensable for a monetary union to function. Historical examples bear this out. It was always a question of political will and the political ability to implement the necessary adjustments. It is thus not only a question of "what is and what should be" but first and foremost a question of will.

Looked at in light of history, "political will" was not only the deciding factor in the creation of the monetary union, it was also crucial for its success. In particular one had to agree on what effect the consequences entailed by a common monetary policy would have on fiscal policy. Two aspects of "political will" are relevant here: either a dominant state, a "hegemon", is accepted that enforces the agreed rules, or one enters into mutual commitments in the form of institutional agreements in order to reduce the risk of "free riders." Economic factors only played a secondary role.

After the efforts towards convergence that took place in the second half of the 1990s, however, "convergence fatigue" set in, bringing with it the failure of the Council of Ministers and the European Commission. Alongside the obliterated budget regulations and growing debt levels, the unpreparedness of individual economies for this level of integration amid increasing economic heterogeneity in the Euro area was clear.

Reasons for the Crisis

Thus we can already identify the reasons for the crisis. They are, however, complex. Today Europe is the focus of international attention. There are doubts about whether European decision makers are getting to grips with the crisis in convincing way, and these doubts are fed by the fact that Europe is currently presenting an image of helplessness on the international stage. And in all this Europe is "only" part of an ongoing and unresolved global crisis. Neither the global financial crisis nor the economic crisis has been overcome. The structural problems in many advanced economies on both sides of the Atlantic are obscured by a frightening amount of sovereign debt and an extremely lax monetary policy. The global financial system and the global economy remain vulnerable, and at the same time enormous economic and financial burdens, particularly for future generations, are being amassed by the misconduct of the generation that today wields political and economic power.

It is indisputable that the way in which the crisis is managed and its solution will be crucial for the future of the economic and monetary union, for Europe itself, for its future economic development, and for its role in the world. In this respect the crisis in Europe has many dimensions:

• it is a crisis of public finances that was foreseeable;

• it is a structural crisis of individual sovereign economies who have lost their price competitiveness, were insufficiently prepared for the conditions of a monetary union, or who have not adapted to it;

• and it is an identity crisis and a crisis of confidence about European integration. As such it addresses the old, unanswered question about the final form integration should take.

A series of flawed developments and infringements of rules and laws was tolerated for political reasons. In their cumulative effect they achieved the proportions of a crisis. No one should say that timely warnings were not given. But in the opinion of those politically responsible there was no pressing need for action or decision making.

• Rules were not monitored. Rules were disregarded and deliberately wrecked.

• The expected effect of peer pressure did not happen.

• For political reasons we embarked upon monetary union with too many countries, a union whose sustainable economic convergence was highly questionable.

• Almost all Member States practised "creative accounting" with regard to their statistics, or else the statistics were simply falsified.

• And clearly most Member States were not aware of

what a common currency meant for them. By definition neither a nominal exchange rate nor a monetary policy are available to individual Member States in a monetary union as a means of adjustment. In the absence of significant cross-border labor mobility in the Euro area, as well as financial transfers, adjustments take place via other means, that is via relative prices. That means via salaries and costs.

Paradigm Shift

The political decisions taken in the context of managing the crisis have changed the character of the monetary union fundamentally, or to put it another way: the Maastricht approach was turned on its head. During the crisis management in spring 2010 three basic mistakes were made in breach of this approach. In the ensuing period they led to an ever-increasing liability for the financial commitments of the peripheral countries of the EU, and to a further increase in the costs of crisis management which will ultimately focus on the dwindling number of countries and economies that are (still) economically sound.

1. In financing Greece's program via other Member States (the bailout) in May 2010 and in implementing the program within the monetary union a central, regulatory principle of the Maastricht Treaty was infringed, namely that of states' responsibility for their own sovereign debt. Greece needed a program backed

by the International Monetary Fund and the EU. But the implementation including the financial support by European partners and the IMF ought to have taken place outside the Euro area. This would have set an example that any state that behaves inappropriately within a currency union and thus acts without a sense of solidarity with the common currency, thus getting into difficulties, receives no financial aid as per the "no bailout" clause. In any case support is possible through the EU Balance of Payments Facility which is intended for the use of non-members of the Euro area.

2. The purchase of government bonds on the secondary market by the ECB conflicts with the ban on monetary public sector financing. It is true that interventions in the secondary market are not prohibited, and they were justified by the ECB for monetary reasons, but in practice this is an example of the implementation of fiscal policy. The purchase of government securities under these circumstances means the central bank is funding national budgets. At the same time the central bank through its own action is blurring the areas of responsibility between monetary and fiscal policy, and in so doing is jeopardizing the bank's independent status.

3. The creation of an initially temporary financial stability facility and then of a permanent funding "mechanism" for countries in difficulties. Through this, Member States take on liability for the debts of other states, which in extreme cases, for example a sovereign

bankruptcy or a state's withdrawal from the monetary union, leads to *de facto* financial transfers.

Thus the regulatory principles of the economic and monetary union have not only been treated in a lax manner, they have been disregarded. The regulatory principles and the rules of monetary policy were regarded in particular by political actors and commentators who were not "handicapped" by regulatory policy as formulae that could be interpreted flexibly, and not as central regulatory stipulations. Principles and rules that should be regarded as guidelines for political action at all times and not only in "fair weather" were regarded as onerous, as they restrict the political sphere of maneuver. But it is precisely during times of crisis that such principles should provide some orientation in the medium term. We can see here clear differences in legal understanding and sense of right and wrong between the Member States and within the European institutions.

Crisis Management

The overcoming of the crisis needed a comprehensive approach and further steps on the road to "political union." As we have already seen, the term "political union" has always remained vague. If its understanding during the negotiations over the Maastricht Treaty was still based on a common foreign and security policy and domestic and legal policy, in the second half of the 1990s the Stability Pact was defined as part of this political union. Today the term is understood as the extension of monetary union by means of a fiscal union or more.

Overcoming the crisis means addressing four points:

1. Stabilization and reduction of public debt. In this context the consolidation of public finances is indispensable. The current austerity debate and the discussion about growth versus consolidation are altogether excessive. The high levels of public debt are themselves already a barrier to growth. Austerity already exists in the countries covered by the program, but in the states that are currently leading the debate in Europe efforts to "save" have not even begun. Debt reduction will not be possible through growth alone. But increased growth cannot be financed by even more debt. What we need is sustainable growth, and thus a reorganization of public finances, a substantial assessment of public responsibilities, and a strategy that takes forward structural reform in the national economies. Budget consolidation and structural reform must go hand in hand.

2. In light of the longer-term effects of the financial and economic crisis in terms of the levels and growth rates of production potential, structural reforms remain central, in particular in the labor and product markets. Many national economies must recover their competitiveness. In a monetary union, as we have already seen, this is only possible through salary and costs adjustments.

This takes time. However, according to the most recent research structural reforms can have positive effects on growth even in the short term. Nevertheless, even in the case of longer-term effects, this is not a reason to put off reforms. The extended period is already underway. This process is painful but unavoidable. Demands to cushion the adjustment processes by financial transfers or interventions by the ECB lead in the wrong direction and resolve neither the structural problems nor the solvency problems of the states in crisis.

3. The restructuring and recapitalization of the banking sector, where necessary. A functioning financial sector that guarantees an efficient allocation of capital is a condition of a sustainable increase in growth. The experience of Japan's "lost decade" has made it particularly clear what consequences can emerge if determined and credible action is not forthcoming. Europe has already lost valuable time here, which is linked since the start of the crisis to the political taboo surrounding the withdrawal of banks from the market.

4. Institutional reforms at supranational level have been instigated. The institutional framework was strengthened by a reform of the Stability and Growth Pact, a new procedure for macroeconomic monitoring, the Fiscal Pact, and a long-term crisis mechanism (European Stability Mechanism). These measures, with the exception of the ESM, point in the right direction, and signify a bit more movement towards "political union." However the focus must lie with the reforms

undertaken at national level. The height of the "firewall" is of secondary importance. For the market operators (and the states in crisis) the amount is always too small, for the governments and parliaments responsible it is always too high.

What should be the ECB's role in all this? The central bank has already taken a very active role in crisis management, and, to put it diplomatically, has stretched its mandate to the limits. Since the boundaries between monetary policy and budgetary policy have become blurred, the ECB must be careful to maintain its independence. The problems in the Euro area are not phenomena that might be combatted using instruments of monetary policy. Doubtless the central bank must take care that banks do not become insolvent through insufficient liquidity. In this respect measures to promote liquidity are completely justified, albeit the provision of liquidity should always be short-term in order to avoid creating distortions on the money markets and interbank markets, and not to limit the flexibility of the central bank through its own actions. The ECB must concentrate on what it can actually achieve. That is the fulfillment of its core mandate. Any discussion about widening the mandate is a distraction from the actual task of guaranteeing price stability. Additional tasks add to the bank's conflicting goals: in such a case its political decisions must be given a particular justification by weighing up different goals one against the other, and its independence is thus undermined.

Quo Vadis, Europe?

What direction will or should Europe's development take? Decisions at the level of heads of state or government on more binding economic coordination and the adherence to tighter budgetary rules were taken more and more frequently. These were *ad hoc* decisions that were combined *ex post* into an "approach" and most recently were complemented by new initiatives under the rubrics of fiscal union and banking union. In this way the debate about a necessary enlargement of the monetary union and with it further steps towards integration has been re-opened.

In the past every step towards integration demanded intensive preparation, thinking about the future, the combination of various theoretical and political approaches, and finally the determination "to lay the foundations of an ever closer union among the peoples of Europe" (Preamble, Treaty on the Functioning of the European Union). In any case, crises always created a motor towards further integration without the existence of a long-term approach let alone clarity about the final form of the process of integration. This was done by adopting the "Schuman Method" of moving forward pragmatically, and of making "mandatory" what was achievable.

The political tensions within the EU and the Euro area, changing political power relationships and increasing economic and fiscal heterogeneity between

Member States in the Euro area make it more difficult than before to reach agreement about the next steps towards integration. It is impossible to ignore the trend towards a re-nationalization of political action. This not only weakens Europe's role in the world and European integration's effectiveness as a role model for other world regions, but can also lead to a threat of disintegration that must be taken seriously. We must tackle this.

What would be the possible options for the future of the monetary union?

a) A return to the spirit and consensus of Maastricht to create a union based on stability, by redressing the flawed developments that have taken place since 1998, and concentrating on maintaining principles and rules.
b) Consolidation of the Euro area in concert with (a).
c) Enlargement of the monetary union by means of a fiscal and banking union as the next steps towards integration.
d) A quantum leap from a union of states to a federal state with central European decision-making institutions for economic and financial policy and hence a full union of liabilities and a transfer union.

Without going into details about these options we must first secure the degree of integration already achieved. This does not mean giving an absolute guarantee regarding the composition of countries in the Euro area as it stands today. This can of course also entail an enlargement. A consolidation of the Euro area seems unavoidable if one wants to maintain the core.

Securing the degree of integration already achieved as a basis for future steps requires at least two basic preconditions:

• A sustainable strengthening of the institutional framework and

• Intensifying democratic control over the process of integration.

In my opinion the steps taken towards more integration are not enough to provide sustainable strengthening of the institutional framework. We must sound a warning against illusory solutions in particular. This applies to rules that appear stringent at first but that in their legal and technical implementation are once again significantly diluted. This applies to rules whose non-adherence is insufficiently sanctioned. Why should the new rules work better than the old ones? This applies also to the debate about Eurobonds, that do not help solve the states' structural problems, that would contravene the no-bailout clause, and for which there is no democratic legitimation.

The creation of a fiscal union would doubtless be an important step towards increased political union. However the ideas and definitions about what that might mean diverge enormously. Fiscal union should be understood neither as a huge European budget with its own EU tax system, nor as the harmonization of the revenue and expenditure structures of the Member States. Both would presuppose a Treaty amendment: the first would even require a European constitution as well as constitutional amendments at national level, as in this case it is a question of the reassignment of responsibilities at national and supra-national level.

A fiscal union should refer exclusively to the institutional framework, and the Fiscal Pact is moving in this direction. My suggestion is the creation of a European Budget Office, initially on an informal basis. Independent experts should deal with Member States' budget planning and the basic assumptions of medium-term planning, and should supervise the implementation of the budget. The findings of the experts in the Budget Office should be made available to the European Commission, the Euro Member States, and the public, and recommendations made to the Commission and the European Council. This could put the notion of peer pressure on a new footing. The Ministers would be able to take a more critical stance with regard to the findings of the Budget Office. This informal committee could become the nucleus of a European Finance Ministry, who would have powers of intervention into national budgetary activities up to an agreed date. In light of events since 1998 and in particular during the crisis, I believe that extremely wide-reaching powers of intervention are urgent if we are to implement the budgetary discipline necessary for a monetary union. However there are various approaches hidden within the idea of a banking union (or even a union of financial markets), which can ultimately lead to a union of liability and a transfer union, and even to a delegation of sovereign rights. A centralized European bank monitoring organization makes sense for institutions with cross-border activities. However, whether centralized monitoring would have avoided the banking risks being taken in Spain, or would have found out about them earlier, remains doubtful. In any case other elements are being discussed such as a European winding-down regime which would have to be able to draw on the required funds in the case of the restructuring and winding-down of banks; or a common investment insurance that in crisis situations would actually lead to direct transfers. These steps must not be taken in a hurry but rather must be well thought out, especially with regard to the financial implications.

Europe made progress in its crisis management. But a further escalation of the crisis could not be avoided. This is linked to the panic-stricken decisions of Spring 2010 that led in the wrong direction, cancelling out and turning upside down central points of the Maastricht Treaty by means of intergovernmental agreements. To overcome the crisis, reforms made at national level remain the central point. However the public's acceptance of this approach is not particularly marked and in many cases it is decidedly negative. Before European solidarity can be called for, we must look to self-help in the form of national solidarity. When the wrong economic policy has been pursued for decades, with national economies living beyond their means for too long, postponing necessary reforms, and continuing to deny the existence of accumulated problems, painful cutbacks are unavoidable. These reforms are in the interest of each country involved. They must make a particular effort to manage the process of adjustment.

Both the Euro and the economic and monetary union have a future: the question is in what form. After over 60 years of successful European integration, which was nevertheless continually characterized by stasis and setbacks, it is worth maintaining this level of integration. This does not have to mean defending the composition of the Euro area at any price. But Europe must show that it is capable of reform. The crisis in the Euro area, which has its roots in the infringement of agreed rules, in the lack of political will, or in the refusal of individual Member States to adjust to the conditions of the monetary union, led to a very difficult and painful road to reform.

The reforms at supra-national level are an attempt to consolidate integration—the first attempt since 1991/93 and the signing of the Maastricht Treaty. Officially a policy of "both–and" is being pursued, that is both consolidation and expansion. In practice, after the introduction of the Euro, another paradigm shift has taken place that aims at expansion. This politically desirable and necessary expansion led to relative disintegration. The framework of the economic union was neglected and never fully implemented. Now is the time to correct this. The important questions are: what do we need to bring about consolidation? What is politically desirable? What is constitutionally possible?

This essay is based on the lecture given by Prof. Jürgen Stark at Convoco Forum on July 28, 2012 in Salzburg.

ROLAND BERGER

GROWTH THROUGH PRIVATELY FINANCED INVESTMENTS IN INFRASTRUCTURE AS THE WAY BACK TO A MORE LEGITIMATE COMMUNITY OF STATES

Amid all the reasoned arguments about the legal constitution of Europe's future economic and financial policy, we are in danger of losing sight of finding a solution that gets us out of the crisis and at the same time returns us to a legitimate state of affairs. In this essay I shall present a program that demonstrates a legitimate and pragmatic route back to a position of legality: growth through privately financed investments in infrastructure. This solution represents the third pillar of a solid program for rescuing the Euro and the EU, and is also an elaboration of the thesis on sovereign debt and insolvency that I published in the 2010 Convoco Edition.

1. What We Have: Conventional Concepts for Reducing Excessive Sovereign Debt

The debate surrounding the insolvency of Greece or other southern European EU states is so topical and urgent that my research findings of two years ago might mistakenly be seen as commonplace today: I stated then that national bankruptcies, that is the situation where a country can no longer pay back its legally undisputed debts, are a realistic possibility and not even a rarity. In reality the threat has become even clearer today: a threat to the cohesion of the monetary union, perhaps even a threat to the cohesion of the EU itself.

It is clear that the sovereign debt and currency crisis restricts our ability to act freely in the economic and also in the political domain. It puts our competitiveness and our prosperity at risk, but equally our unity and ability to act together as Europeans. For this reason it is all the more interesting to see which of the roads that I described in theory are now being embarked upon in order to bring down sovereign debt. Here are just a few thoughts on this.

• National bankruptcy? Up till now we have, thankfully, been able to prevent this in Greece, but also in Ireland and Portugal.

• An orderly restructuring of debt? In the case of Greece, we have at least begun this process, working alongside the International Monetary Fund (IMF). Let us remind ourselves: during the debt reduction of March 2012 private creditors, that is banks, insurers, and funds, gave up claims amounting to 107 billion Euros. Since then the troika of the EU, the European Central Bank (ECB), and the IMF are monitoring whether the government in Athens is fulfilling its related obligations. The necessity of a further round of debt reduction—this time with the additional participation of public-sector creditors—cannot be ruled out, to put it mildly.

• Rigorous budgetary and austerity policies? The bailout fund of the ESM and the Fiscal Pact are certainly important and correct steps: the promise of collective aid on the one hand, and austerity, budgetary, and restructuring obligations, as well as related controls and sanctions on the other. These measures are indispensable, if not universally welcome all to the same extent. They can only succeed if we lobby convincingly and straightforwardly in their favor, without closing our eyes to the social upheavals that accompany them. Moreover, when we realize that it is primarily businesses that create growth and jobs, a look at a highly topical index produced by the World Bank offers encouraging reading. Each year "Ease of Doing Business" describes how the conditions for business in 185 countries are developing. Most recently in this listing Greece has risen from 89th place to 78th, and Italy from 75th to 73rd, no less. Ireland has climbed from 16th to 15th, while Portugal remains in 30th place. This shows that efforts at reform are manifesting small signs of success, albeit early ones.

• Suspend the independence of central banks and print money in order to "inflate away" the debt? This is where the argument rages most fiercely. To what extent has the ECB maintained its independence since it announced it intended to buy a theoretically unlimited amount of sovereign debt belonging to crisis states, albeit subject to conditions and on the secondary market? The bank invokes Article 18 of its statute, according to which the ECB is allowed to buy or sell "marketable instruments." Government bonds are marketable instruments, but does this also apply to bonds offered by crisis states? In addition this proviso in the ECB statute does not seem created for the purpose of stabilizing the price of bonds issued by vulnerable Euro states. Until now, of course, inflation has been kept in check; but in the case of many countries it has already arrived in the shape of "asset inflation." Will the ECB manage to bring general inflation down again below the target of 2% through the promised reduction in the liquidity that has been created? Historically something like this has often been promised, but as yet it has never been achieved.

• Debt reduction through economic growth? Until now this has always ended badly in Europe as every general program of "just saving", every austerity program, every internal devaluation by means of budget, wage, and price reductions is always linked to recession. We can and must think more creatively in order to break free of this cycle. I will return to this theme in particular later on.

Even in the future a general ban on borrowing will not be a suitable measure, as there are also "good" debts—albeit at the moment they are not sovereign, but private and belong to credit-worthy investors—that finance genuine investments, thereby boosting growth and resulting in a return on the investment. It is thus the combination of growth-oriented economic policy and substantial budgetary consolidation that could prove to be the best road to sustainable success.

2. What We Need: Growth and Confidence

An intelligent balance is what matters, but unfortunately in the third year of the European sovereign debt and monetary crisis politicians are increasingly limiting their programs for rescuing the Euro to just two packages of measures: "austerity" for the crisis states and "financing" for the (still) productive Member States of northern Europe, and for Germany in particular. Both are correct and necessary, but are not enough to prevent the disintegration of the common currency and perhaps even of the European Union itself. In the meantime narrowing the options down to austerity and financial aid has taken Europe into a threefold crisis:

• First, the sovereign debt crisis and the Euro crisis have intensified.

• Second, the economies of both the Eurozone and of the EU in general have in the meantime gone into recession, led by the crisis states with their austerity programs, which sometimes recall the experience of Germany in the 1920s.

• Third, European integration is experiencing a serious political crisis. Because of their shrinking economies the crisis states are suffering from growing unemployment, asset destruction, and social tensions. Some of the media in these countries talk about "diktats" from Brussels forcing them into poverty. The citizens of the still financially strong "northern countries" think (wrongly but understandably) that they are being propelled into risking their savings in order to help their neighbors pay off debts accumulated through "unsound economic activity." Europe is deeply divided.

Economic growth would be what is needed to re-build the confidence European citizens place in their currency and in their union. State-financed growth programs are out of the question: on the one hand state growth programs would require more sovereign debt; on the other they would not solve the growth crisis, as it is not a question of an economic crisis but rather a structural crisis affecting our competitiveness, which can only be overcome via structural reforms including reductions in expenditure, salaries, and costs.

3. What We Can Do: Growth Through Privately Financed Investments in Infrastructure

A way out of this crisis is offered by a growth program that is politically monitored but privately financed and that functions within the market economy, a program for creating and strengthening as well as modernizing Europe's infrastructure. To do this the cost in the EU alone is estimated to be at least one billion Euros. And it is estimated that there are 170 billion Euros available worldwide in private wealth to finance this. The job of the politicians, I suggest, would be to bring these infrastructure needs together with the investment requirements of private capital through investor and competition friendly regulation and market-economic, non-ideological, and legally reliable structures for each "investment case."

Right at the top of the list of possible projects is the telecoms infrastructure, which is in need of technological regeneration through broadband information super-highways. European regulation policies from the time of the "Post and Telephony Monopoly" are still preventing the necessary investments from paying off. Major telecoms providers such as France Télécom, Deutsche Telekom, or Telefonica are not able to mobilize private capital. If politicians made up their mind in favor of innovative regulation suitable for the capital markets, this could produce considerable growth: with investments of more than 270 billion Euros in the communications infrastructure this might not only create several hundred thousand jobs in Europe, but it could also increase the productivity of users in private business and public administration. In addition, a European information and Internet industry might develop, such as the USA has made possible in the form of Google, Amazon, and Facebook.

In the energy industry, too, we have not been leveraging all our potential for a long time now. In Europe over the coming years—particularly after the German turnaround on energy—220 billion Euros must be invested in networks and storage facilities. This presumes the existence of a European energy policy and corresponding long-term planning. Neither is currently in place.

In the area of water supply and waste water management Europe has an investment backlog of at least 200 billion Euros. And in European road construction the investment required is estimated to be 180 billion Euros.

Unfortunately Europe's dominant ideology says that infrastructure should reside in the hands of the state, with strange divergences between the countries: for example, in France the water supply is private, but the state provides the electricity. By contrast in Germany the water supply must come from the state while electricity is largely provided by the private sector. In many countries there exist privately financed toll roads, while only in a transit country such as Germany this is not allowed for some reason.

Thus an infrastructure program, at least partly privately financed as a market-economic growth plan for Europe, could be the missing third pillar of a solid Euro rescue program—alongside structural change through austerity for better competitiveness and budgetary discipline (not only) in the south, and bridge financing provided in the spirit of solidarity by Germany and other northern European Member States in order to reassure the financial markets.

In this way, in the middle of a crisis, Europe could create a highly innovative and productive economy with excellent infrastructure. The private suppliers would profit from growth and increased productivity, and the workers would profit from more and qualitatively high-grade jobs. At the same time, with increased tax revenue and reduced welfare costs, sovereign debt would be reduced. Even people's confidence in the Euro and in European integration would be restored.

SHAUKAT AZIZ
A PLEA FOR "GOOD GOVERNANCE"

In the world in which we live, a constantly-changing, interconnected, and aspirational world, we have for the last few years been hearing more and more about governance, and with it, good governance and bad governance. These terms have become so ubiquitous that they are now entrenched in the rhetoric of modern development, and as such have almost lost their meaning for ordinary people. This is a pity, and something I would like to reverse, as I am a passionate believer in the very concept of good governance, and its fundamental necessity to the healthy development of emerging societies and economies.

Without applying the principles of good governance, no government can hope to win the respect and support of its people. Without good governance, no citizen can have faith that his or her rulers are acting in the best interests of the nation and its people. Without good governance, no country can hope to rise above poverty, corruption, nepotism, and totalitarianism into the ranks of modern, world-class nation states, and take a place among the community of nations that stand hand-in-hand against these very basic cruelties to mankind. No government that ignores the need for good governance can hope to become a true leader of its own people, bequeathing to them a thriving, open, accountable, and healthy democracy—which I believe is the birthright of every man and woman. Indeed, good governance lies at the heart of every successful nation, every successful economy, every successful and thriving democracy. Good governance is the bedrock of modern civilization.

My faith in good governance is rooted in my own hands-on experience in Pakistan, where I was Prime Minister and Finance Minister between 1999 and 2007. It is my profound belief that the principles of good governance mirror the hopes and expectations of the citizens of all countries, and that, when delivered via a set of legitimate rules and regulations, they can unleash the latent potential of even the most corrupt and impoverished societies. It is the common aspiration of all people to have a say in their own destiny, and it is through good governance that this right is delivered.

Good governance cannot be delivered in part; it can only come about as the result of a cohesive, comprehensive, integrated, and systematic approach. It may be difficult to deliver in its entirety—human nature being what it is. It may need constant vigilance to ensure it becomes an integral part of a society's fabric. But the delivery of good governance as the result of a set of pre-conditions must be the goal if the deserving citizens of the world's emerging economies are to live in peace and prosperity, and with the knowledge that their government can and will deliver a better life for future generations.

There are many international and national organizations and institutions dedicated to the good governance cause, and many of them provide assistance, aid, and loans to help governments introduce reforms that take them along the path towards good governance. Many also withhold or delay this help, be it in kind or cash, if they are unsatisfied with the progress, which is constantly monitored, being made by the governments they sponsor. This they do in the hope of incentivizing governments to remain true to the goal of good governance.

There are a number of components of good governance that can be easily understood in isolation. Each has merit in its own right, but achieving each would be difficult, if not impossible, without the others. I will outline here the components of good governance that I believe are vital parts of the whole. Many are self-explanatory, and form the basis of what many people in the developed world are able to take for granted—good governance.

The most important component contributing to the emergence of good governance in any country is democracy. There is no alternative to representation of, by, and for the people. Democracy has come under attack in recent years, especially as the world deals with the excesses that led to the financial crisis that first struck the West and has spread to the rest of the world. But it should be noted that while it was a lack of regulation in a complex and fast-moving financial industry that was at the root of the problems the world is facing, the fact is that the problems that led to it are being uncovered, dealt with, and redressed in countries that are constantly undergoing self-examination as part of their attempts to improve their systems of governance and oversight. It is the mark of a mature citizenry that its members are able to look themselves collectively in the mirror, and honestly identify their own faults as a society, rather than blame their problems on others. The desire for constant progress, development, and improvement is the hallmark of a mature, democratic society. Contrarily, defensiveness, the inability to admit to faults or take the criticism of others, mark out a government that is immature and unworthy of rule, and one that ultimately will be called upon to answer to the people it has exploited and abused in order to perpetuate its own often corrupt and inept rule.

As the UN's Economic and Social Commission for Asia and the Pacific has pointed out so eloquently, "representative democracy does not necessarily mean that the concerns of the most vulnerable in society would be taken into consideration in decision making. Participation needs to be informed and organized. This means freedom of association and expression on the one hand and an organized civil society on the other hand."

With representative government as the "key cornerstone" of good governance, other component parts must be introduced to strengthen, support, and perpetuate it.

Before getting to these component parts of good governance, let me first make it clear that a government intent on introducing reforms needs a clear strategic vision for each individual sector, strategies that can be communicated to the people in a way that is easy to understand. This is fundamental to popular participation. If the people of a country do not understand the very concepts by which they are ruled, those concepts can have neither credibility nor clout, and will not achieve long-term success. It is a vital part of good governance that the people being governed feel ownership of and participation in the process by which their country is run.

Once the strategy is in place, policies and then implementation follow, in that order. Many governments make the mistake of starting out with grand plans without having first set strategic goals for each sector, be it health, education, energy, tourism, arts, industry, finance, defense, the judiciary, diplomacy, or security both internal and external. The overall strategic agenda for each sector must highlight its strengths and weaknesses, leveraging the strengths and improving the weaknesses.

This clear strategic view gives rise to policies; that is, the "how to" of achieving the strategic goal. Moving from the macro—understanding the challenges and requirements of reform at a broad level—to the micro, these policies then need to be put into action. Only with this sequential methodology can any country deliver on its strategic goals, and achieve the good governance that underpins a mature and healthy nation, that respects and is, in turn, respected by its citizenry.

Good governance requires the participation and agreement of the people; it requires accountability, transparency, equality, and inclusion; it needs the rule of law and the independence of the judiciary, and the criminalization of corruption. Good governance can take root only when government steps back to allow civil society and private enterprise to work under their own steam, and with oversight by independent regulators that are not answerable to or influenced by the government, in either deed or perception. Good governance ensures all people have a voice and that their voices are heard. It guarantees protection for society's most vulnerable. With good governance, nations move with the times, incorporating new technology that improves efficiency and reduces, and hopefully eventually eliminates the roadblocks of red tape, unleashing the forces and potential of society.

Let's take a simple, hypothetical example. Let's say the government of an emerging country decides to encourage the development of a tourism industry in order to create jobs, generate revenues, and improve the national image. It is not the job of the government to become a tourism operator; it is the job of the government to encourage the participation of the private sector in the development of every aspect of a tourism industry. Government won't build the hotels, but it can create an enabling environment by, for instance, allotting parcels of land for sale or auction to developers who will build the hotels, thereby taking a moribund asset, the land, and enabling its transformation into an active asset that creates jobs, generates tax revenue, and caters for a hoped-for influx of tourists.

Delivery is the end game. To get there, the other component parts must be achieved.

To take the tourism example further, the land can be sold in a public auction that is broadcast live on television. The auction takes place after a set time during which anyone who wishes to can examine the conditions of the sale. An independent media can cover the auction, report on all aspects of the sale process. Organizers and buyers can be scrutinized. Members of the public and their representatives can attend the auction. Anyone who has any opinion about the process can have their voice heard—they can complain to the government's tourism department, to the parliamentary committee that oversees the tourism industry. The government can encourage private sector involvement via a liberal visa policy, a free market for travel operators, airlines, hotels. Independent regulators will then oversee the industry to ensure the public interest is protected.

Institutions involved in the structural reform and development of every sector should ensure that all queries and complaints are dealt with in a time deemed reasonable, thus entrenching their accountability. The government has responsibility here to ensure that independent regulators provide oversight for each sector, as central banks do, for instance, over financial industry. But the business of government is not business; it is the facilitation of fair, open, and accountable business that benefits the country with appropriate supervisions to protect public interest.

The entire process should be open, transparent, easily understood; all players should be accountable to the people through parliamentary process, independent regulation, and media scrutiny. Every aspect of the sale of the government land to private developers in this example of tourism should be free of cronyism, and be seen to be free of cronyism. To ensure this is the case, the judiciary must be independent, every citizen must be equal before the law, have equal access to justice, and trust in the application of the law by an impartial and incorruptible police force. The law must also be the upholder of all rights for the citizenry, including the basic human rights of freedoms of speech, movement, association, and religion. All people must feel the law exists in their service.

This leads to the criminalization of bribery—both the giving and receiving of bribes should be punishable by the severe application of anti-corruption laws. Every nation should sign up to and ratify the United Nations Convention Against Corruption, thereby signaling to rest of the world their determination to prevent corruption, strengthen international law enforcement and cooperative judicial practices, as well as provide effective legal mechanisms for asset recovery. Bad money doesn't deserve a home, so banks should never be permitted to accept deposits that cannot be traced to a legitimate source. Due diligence, transparency, and accountability should be integral facets of the financial industry as a way of limiting and, hopefully, eradicating bribery and corruption that as we have seen is a pillar industry of many emerging economies.

One way of ensuring an immediate impact on corruption levels is to pay civil servants decent salaries so they can enjoy a comfortable life and provide for their own retirement. For people to behave and perform responsibly, they must be paid well. When they retire, they should be able to afford to live in the manner to which they have become accustomed. Otherwise, efficiency is not maximized and corruption is encouraged—and all the evils of bad governance creep into the system.

Elected representatives must have passion and vision, and clear benchmarks on how they will deliver on the promises they make about the areas for which they have responsibility. Processes and institutions must produce results that meet the needs of each society, while making the best use of all resources at their disposal. The concept of efficiency in the context of good governance also covers the sustainable use of natural resources and protection of the environment. It also includes the use of new technology to ensure best international practice at every level, further enhancing efficiency.

I believe that human contact should be removed from areas where it can be a hindrance to efficiency and honesty. The introduction of electronic communication removes the possibility of bribery—giving and taking—from the process of taxation, for instance, and maximizes the likelihood that private individuals, companies, and corporations will pay the correct tax. Here, there should be random audits of 10 percent of returns, based on specific criteria. Tax receipts would go up; corruption, to a large extent, would be reduced; harassment by government officials would fall. A reduction in contact between officials and citizens would have immediate results.

To conclude a necessarily brief outline of my views on good governance, let me note that the best ways to boost efficiency and reduce corruption are structural reform, liberalization, deregulation, and privatization. The more a country deregulates, the more it releases the forces and potential of the private sector and civil society. There is no reason to have government involvement in private business.

This does not mean abdication by the government. Government must encourage the establishment of independent regulators. The role of regulators is much more important in a deregulated market as they must know their specific sectors inside and out. So sector-specific regulators—with fixed terms, so they are not answerable to politicians and thus can build clout and credibility—become a vital component of the good governance model.

Governments should create an enabling environment and then let go. The private sector and civil society have enough capacity to conduct their own affairs; with independent oversight which is key. Their ability to contribute to the creation of strong, stable, prosperous, and democratic societies will depend on the strategic vision of governments that have the best interests of the people as their guiding force.

LIST OF ABBREVIATIONS

TFEU	Treaty on the Functioning of the European Union
BDI	Federation of German Industry [Bundesverband der Deutschen Industrie e.V.]
GDP	Gross Domestic Product
ECOFIN	Economic and Financial Affairs Council
EEG	Erneuerbare-Energien-Gesetz [German Renewable Energy Act]
EFSF	European Financial Stability Facility
ESFS	European System of Financial Supervision
ESM	European Stability Mechanism
EU	European Union
EEC	European Economic Community
EMU	European Economic and Monetary Union
ECB / ESCB	European Central Bank/European System of Central Banks
GG	Grundgesetz der Bundesrepublik Deutschland [German Constitution]
GWB	Gesetz gegen Wettbewerbsbeschränkungen [Restriction of Competition Act]
IMF	International Monetary Fund
UNC	United Nations Charter
UN	United Nations

AUTHORS AND PARTICIPANTS

His Excellency Shaukat Aziz was Prime Minister of Pakistan from 2004 to 2007, following five years as Finance Minister. After graduating from Gordon College, Rawalpindi in 1967, Mr. Aziz gained an MBA degree from the Institute of Business Administration, University of Karachi. Starting as an intern at Citibank Aziz later became Executive Vice President and held several senior management positions including Head of Institutional Banking for Central Eastern Europe, the Middle East and Africa and later for Asia Pacific, followed by Chief Executive of the bank's global wealth management business. He was named "Finance Minister of the Year" for 2001 by *Euromoney* and *The Bankers* magazine. Mr. Aziz restored his country's credibility at home and abroad. His policies were based on the principals of liberalization, deregulation and privatization, accompanied by strong regulatory oversight. His tenor was marked by high economic growth and reduction in poverty. Mr. Aziz co-chaired the UN Secretary General's Committee to promote reform and coherence at the United Nations. In recognition of his services to Pakistan, he was awarded an Honorary Doctor of Law by his Alma Mater, The Institute of Business Administration, University of Karachi, Pakistan. Mr. Aziz is a member of several boards and advisory boards of various commercial and non-profit entities around the world.

Prof. Dr. h.c. Roland Berger is the founder and Chairman of the Supervisory Board of Roland Berger Strategy Consultants, Munich. He completed his studies in business administration in Munich and Hamburg. From 1971 to 1972, he taught marketing and advertising at the Technical University of Munich. He has been a visiting professor since 1996 and an honorary professor for business administration and management consultancy at the Brandenburg Technical University in Cottbus since 2000. He is a member of the board of governors of the Ludwig-Maximilian University and the University of Music and Theatre in Munich, sits on the board of trustees of the ifo Institute for Economic Research at Munich University and the board of the INSEAD Business School. He is also a member of many international advisory committees and supervisory boards. Since 2008, he has been Chairman of the Board of Trustees of the Roland Berger Foundation.

Dr. Corinne Michaela Flick studied both law and literature, taking American studies as her subsidiary. She gained her Dr. Phil. in 1989. She has worked as in-house lawyer for Bertelsmann Buch AG and Amazon.com. In 1998 she became General Partner in Vivil GmbH und Co. KG, Offenburg. She is Founder and Chair of the Convoco Foundation.

Dr. Flick is Chair of the Board of Trustees of the Aspen Institute, Germany, Co-Founder of the Friends of the Bavarian State Library, Munich, and a member of the

Executive Committee of the International Council of the Tate Gallery, London.

Prof. Dr. Christoph G. Paulus was awarded his LL.M. at Berkeley. He studied law in Munich, taking his doctorate in law in 1980. His habilitation, gained in 1991, was in Civil Law, Civil Procedure and Roman Law, for which he was awarded the Medal of the University of Paris II. In 1989–90 he was in receipt of a Feodor Lynen Stipend from the Humboldt Foundation in Berkeley. In 1992–94 he was Associate Professor at Augsburg, and from the summer semester 1994 he was at the Law Faculty of the Humboldt University in Berlin, becoming Dean of the Faculty in 2008–2010. In 2009 he was made Director of the Research Center Institute for Interdisciplinary Restructuring, and Consultant to the International Monetary Fund and the World Bank. Among other roles he is Member (and Director) of the International Insolvency Institute of the American College of Bankruptcy and the International Association for Procedural Law. Since 2006 he has been advisor on insolvency law to the German delegation to UNCITRAL. He is on the editorial board of the *Zeitschrift für Wirtschaftsrecht (ZIP)*, the *Norton Annual Review of International Insolvency*, and the *International Insolvency Law Review*, among other journals.

Prof. Dr. Dr. h.c. Ingolf Pernice studied law in Marburg and Geneva, European studies in Bruges, and economics in Freiburg. He took his doctorate in fundamental rights in the EEC at the University of

Augsburg. From 1980 to 1983 he was an administrator at the European Commission at the DG Competition and from 1983 to 1992 member of the Legal Service. He received his postdoctoral qualification at Bayreuth University in 1987, on equity in public law. Co-founder and co-editor of the *European Journal of Business Law*. From 1993 to 1996 Professor for Public, European, and International Law at the Johann Wolfgang Goethe-Universität, Frankfurt. In 1996 Professor at the Humboldt-University, Berlin. Appointed by the European Commission member of the European Forum for Environment and Sustainable Development. Founder of the Walter Hallstein-Institute for European Constitutional Law of the Humboldt-University and Founder of the European Constitutional Law Network. He organizes the lecture series forum constitutionis europeae (FCE) and the Humboldt Lectures on Europe (HRE). From 1998 to 2004 Dean of International Relations at the Humboldt-University Law Faculty; and from 2006 to 2008 Dean of the Law Faculty. Since 1999 Editor of *Schriftenreihe Europäisches Verfassungsrecht* and member of the advisory board of the Columbia Journal of European Law. He is member of the boards and advisory boards of many law journals. He obtained a doctorate *honoris causa* from the New Bulgarian University, Sofia, in 2006 and was awarded the Cross of Merit on Ribbon of The Order of Merit of the Federal Republic of Germany in 2008. He represented the German Parliament defending the Treaty of Lisbon in the proceedings of the German Federal Constitutional Court in 2008/09. His special research areas are

European constitutional law, European environmental law, and comparative and global constitutionalism.

Prof. Dr. Dr. h.c. Wolfgang Schön studied law and economics studies at the University of Bonn, and was awarded his doctorate at Bonn in 1985. In 1992 he received his postdoctoral qualification in civil law, commercial, corporate, and tax law in Bonn. He was Professor at the University of Bielefeld from 1992 to 1996, and Director of the Institute for Tax Law and of the Centre of European Commercial Law, Bonn from 1996 to 2002. Since 2002 he has been Director and Scientific Member of the Max Planck Institute for Intellectual Property, Competition, and Tax Law in Munich. He has been Honorary Professor of Civil, Commercial, Corporate, and Tax Law at the Ludwig-Maximilians-University, Munich since 2002. Since 2008 Professor Schön has been Vice-President of the Max Planck Society.

Univ.-Prof. Dr. phil. habil. Hannes Siegrist studied history, sociology, German literature, and journalism at the University of Zurich, receiving his doctorate in 1976. In 1992 he completed his habilitation in Modern History, with particular reference to economic and social history, in the Department of History, Free University Berlin. In 1997 he took up the Chair of Comparative European Cultural and Social History at the Institute of Cultural Science, Faculty of Social Sciences and Philosophy, University of Leipzig.
From 1976 to 1996 he held teaching and research

positions at the University and Center for Interdisciplinary Research in Bielefeld; the University of Zurich; the Free University, Berlin; the European University Institute, Florence; the Swedish Collegium for Advanced Study in the Social Sciences, Uppsala; and the Central European University, Budapest.

Since 1997 he has been Director of the Institute of Cultural Sciences, and Dean of the Faculty of Social Sciences and Philosophy, University of Leipzig, as well as leader of group projects and doctoral programmes. Professor Siegrist advises on various scientific and cultural bodies and edits academic journals, series, and Internet portals on recent European history. In 2001 he was Visiting Professor at the Ecole Normale Supérieure in Paris, and Research Professor at the Social Science Research Center in Berlin in 2004/05. In 2007 he was made a Member of the Saxonian Academy of Sciences in Leipzig.

Prof. Dr. Jürgen Stark studied economics at the universities of Hohenheim and Tübingen and graduated in 1973. He gained a doctorate in economics 1975 and was appointed Honorary Professor at the University of Tübingen in 2005. He was a member of the Executive Board and the Governing Council of the European Central Bank (ECB) from 2006 to 2011, responsible for economics, statistics, and information systems. He resigned from his position in December 2011, thus not completing his term which would have run until 2014. Before joining the ECB, he was Vice-President of the

Deutsche Bundesbank, where he was responsible for European and International Affairs. Prior to this position he served as State Secretary at the German Federal Ministry of Finance and as Personal Representative of the Federal Chancellor in the preparation of G7/G8 Economic Summits for four years. Before that he held various positions at the Ministry of Finance, the Federal Chancellery, and the Federal Ministry of Economics, dealing with national and international monetary and financial issues. His publications include many articles and papers in professional journals on public finances, European monetary integration, institution building, and the global financial system.

Prof. Dr. Pirmin Stekeler-Weithofer studied German, theoretical linguistics, philosophy (MA 1975), and mathematics (Diplom 1977) in Konstanz, Berlin, Prague, and Berkeley. He received his doctorate in 1984, and his postdoctoral qualification in 1987. Since 1992 he has been Professor of Theoretical Philosophy at the University of Leipzig. He has taught and researched widely abroad in Campinas, São Paulo, Brazil(1988), Pittsburgh, PA (1990–92, 2006), Swansea, Great Britain (1997/98), and held the Theodor Heuss Chair in New York (2002). Since 1994 he has been Director of the Humanities Center, and since 2009 Director of the Center for Higher Studies at the University of Leipzig. He has been a member of the Saxonian Academy of Sciences in Leipzig since 1998, and its president since 2008. He is Vice-President of the International Hegel Association and the International Ludwig Wittgenstein

Society. Since 2005 he has been a member of the Selection Committee for Research Grants at the Alexander von Humboldt Foundation.